Acting is Living

*Exploring the Ten Essential Elements
in any Successful Performance.*

Cliff Osmond

Published by Cinevest, Inc.
1526 14th Street, Suite 7
Santa Monica, CA 90404
(310) 393-6022

Editor: Lois Cheraz
Layout & Design: Jon McPhalen

ISBN: 978-0-578-06942-5 (paperback)

Osmond, Cliff, 1937-

Acknowledgments

I wish to thank most especially Dr. Maya Roth, Dr. Jim Miller, Jim Buchanan, and Armand Assante for their early reading of this book. Their dedication, detailed notes on my original scattered manuscript, accompanied by their patience and encouragement, were golden in value.

I would also like to thank John Furia, Jeff Bell, Mari Ferguson, Gary Black, and Shirley King for their willingness to read and offer many comments on subsequent drafts. To Jon McPhalen, I owe my overwhelming gratitude for his creativity, wisdom, taste, and patience in organizing and formatting this book; to Lois Cheraz many, many thanks for her detailed editorial insights and suggestions; to my wife, Gretchen, and my daughter, Mishi, and my son, Eric, may I offer my eternal gratitude for their unending love, encouragement, and creative input; until the day I die my cup of gratitude to them will never be emptied. Finally, to my 20,000 students with whom I have collaborated in this ephemeral world of acting, and who have put up with my suggestions, instructions, theories, my barks, bites, and more than occasional bursts of impatience, I can only hope they have learned from our efforts a small portion of what they have taught me.

To Billy Wilder, Jim Buchanan, and Armand Assante

Their talent speaks volumes; my gratitude is beyond words.

To my wife, Gretchen

For a lifetime of patience and care.

Contents

Part II: The Five Enhancing Elements of Good Acting

Forward

Performing is a selfish journey. As performers, we are the self-appointed ferrymen of the human soul.

Historically, in the film and theater industry, there have been in acting a few noted brilliant "creatures of instinct": the more recent names include Kean, Duse, Magnani, Vissotski, and Brando —plus a few others still evolving. All were fervid practitioners and students of the theater and film, subscribing to teachings historical and contemporary—acting theories that go back 2400 years—still worth reading and as completely applicable today as they were yesterday.

I have been blessed in my life to be influenced by two individuals from two entirely different generations who have taught me and many other actors—scores of whom have achieved giant status in my industry.

When I was a young actor, I was devoted to the teacher Mira Rostova, a fiercely poetic and beautiful woman, an individual of laser-like intelligence. She was a contemporary of the artists and teachers who emerged from the Group Theater in NY: Clurman, Odets, Meisner, Adler, Hagen, and Strasberg.

For the past 25 years, Cliff Osmond has been my mentor, coach, colleague, and co-conspirator on all scripts/performances good, great, and bad. In my estimation, he has defined his own historic destiny as being the most articulate expert in the theater and film industry today, whether that expertise is on the subject of acting, writing, or directing.

People often ask me why so many talented people in the Industry emerged from New York. I have only one answer: we had the teachers. Whosoever occupies that lexicon today, Cliff Osmond is unmatched. He is in a class by himself.

I met Cliff in 1985, soon after my reading a spare, metaphorical screenplay he had written. One year later, we made the script into the film *The Penitent*, with the late, great Raul Julia. We shot it in the harsh landscape of Central Mexico. On set, I found Cliff unusually humble, especially for a man with such a formidable mind and intellect. He was equally incisive in his writing and direction, and his screenplay was wound tight as a bull waiting in a shoot. The journey it and he took us on was an electric ride.

Reading this book, I found it filled with many of the same theories he lives by and promulgates when working with him. It is essentially a book of his very specific precepts that every thinking actor should not only wish to live by, but also should long to be reminded of every day.

Cliff's writing on the dilemma of the actor is an illumination. His book is the distillation of his lifetime; it reflects his thoughts and experiences on the subject of being an actor. The devoted actor will cherish this book.

It is as clear and as welcome as a coherent beam of light.

Armand Assante
New York, NY
August, 2010

Hey, yeah, sweet memories,
We got sweet, sweet memories,
Taking me back,
Taking me back....

from *Sweet Memories*
by Sir Paul McCartney

With Billy Wilder on the set of *Kiss Me, Stupid*

This photo of Billy Wilder shows me, an acolyte, watching the master. He allowed me to be on the set every day, whether I was scheduled to film or not, and later allowed me to sit in while he edited the film. When he gave me this picture, he joked that the photo was emblematic: I was always working, while he concerned himself with more pedestrian pursuits, like the LA Dodgers and the sports page spread out on his personal on-set hammock.

Through my career, whether I was doing a film with him or not (I did four), Billy would make himself available for a visit at his office, or we would go to lunch. We chatted about movies, writing, or the meal in front us. During career down periods, I would think: "If Billy is willing to sit with me, and just talk, I must be worth something. Don't quit. Keep trying." Thank you, Billy.

With Armand Assante on the set of *The Penitent*

I met Armand Assante many years ago because my daughter, at the time in college, was best friends with his sister-in-law. My daughter said she could get my script, *The Penitent*, to him—but I ignored the suggestion for three weeks. When my daughter called again and said, "You know, Papa, that's your problem. You'd have had a better career if you were pushier." I capitulated and sent her the script.

Thus began a wonderfully creative collaboration between us, a deep friendship that continues to this day. Assante's unique on-screen intensity and character complexity—a result of his obsessive attention to preparation and performance details—sets him securely in the passionate acting tradition of such American greats as Barrymore, Garfield, Cagney, Bogart, and Brando.

With Jack Lemmon in *Front Page*

A thorough professional throughout his career, Jack's stumbling, bumbling line readings of a script were impeccably rehearsed and brought to performance only after hours and hours of work, yet in every take he maintained a startling freshness and spontaneity. I had the pleasure of working in three films with Jack.

In spite of many, many hours on the set with him, often seated close-by, sometimes chatting, I never knew him, except for the Jack-the-character he revealed in his various portrayals. Perhaps it was my fault (I was too shy to probe his real feelings), but great actors probably reveal more in their work than they ever do in their private relationships, anyway. Maybe that is as it should be: the actor eventually dies, but the work endures forever.

With Peter Sellers in *Kiss Me, Stupid*

On stage, Peter exhibited the great actor's ability to transform himself, seemingly whole, into any character he was playing. The scene pictured above does not appear in the film as it was shot prior to Peter's first heart attack. Peter was not able to return to the film and was subsequently replaced by Ray Walston.

When I see the photo now, hanging on a wall in my home, I think that somewhere in a vault of one of the studios there is the footage of my extensive work with Peter. Hopefully, some day it can be found because I would like my heirs to see it. It will show me working opposite a genius: an artist, natural, real, brilliant, imaginative, surprising, and dangerous, yet easy to work with. Peter made everyone around him always better than we (most especially, I) deserved to be.

With Jack Lemmon and Shirley MacLaine in *Irma la Douce*

When I think of Shirley MacLaine, I return to my first on-set image of her: very good champagne; bubbly, effervescent, and extremely heady. Performing in my first feature film, *Irma la Douce*, Shirley was unexpectedly gracious, and a warm and sincere hello and an even warmer good-bye bracketed my single day's work with her.

Many, many years later, when we met at a Tony Award® function, Shirley again greeted me with a smile, as if the ensuing forty years had not elapsed. She looked me up and down, the ever-present twinkle still in her eyes, and said, "Where did you go, Cliff?" (I had lost a hundred pounds in the intervening time!) A lady, a charmer, a brilliant actress, a finer human being, Shirley remains the best champagne, getting better with age.

With Carroll O'Connor in *All In The Family*

Arriving on the set to be an episodic guest-star in the midst of Carroll O'Connor's starring galaxy was a challenge. His co-stars, Jean Stapleton, Rob Reiner, and Sally Struthers, had been working on their characters for three years; I was on set for three days. On the second day of rehearsal, I was still unsure of myself and struggled to find my character. Being excellent actors, they expanded their brilliant acting work to fill my void. I asked them to give me one more day to find my legs, and they generously did. The next day, just before shooting, I came up to the mark and balance was achieved. Due to their professionalism, generosity, and talent, the episode remains one of my TV career highlights.

With Kim Novak on the set of *Kiss Me, Stupid*

The fondest memory I have of Kim is her bringing homemade cookies and margaritas at 3 AM for the cast and crew during an all-night shoot at Universal, on a night she was not scheduled to work. She was a consummate pro and a sweetheart to work with throughout the film.

When I see this photo of myself standing relaxed, right hand in pocket, looking off in the distance, casually chatting on set with Kim Novak, I laugh out loud. Casually chatting? It was the best acting I did on or off the film! Kim, with skin as smooth as velvet, and a voice both sultry and warm, was one of the most beautiful and sexy women I had ever met! I was enthralled.

With Cornel Wilde (back turned) in *Shark's Treasure*
(also pictured: Yaphet Kotto and John Neilson)

When my agent first attempted to secure an audition with Cornel Wilde for me to play the Mexican heavy in *Shark's Treasure*, Cornel refused. He wanted a legitimate Spanish-speaking actor and was a known stickler for realism. My agent said he would continue to push for the audition and, ultimately, he did get me a copy of the script. Determined to get the part, I got my favorite book for accent training, *Herman's Manual of Foreign Dialects*, off the shelf, studied maniacally, and met and spoke with a Mexican neighbor every day, studying his manners and gestures. Two weeks later, I read for a reluctant Cornel, who bought this Turk as a Mexican. Never say never "No" to a driven actor!

With Lucille Ball in *Here's Lucy*

I had the good fortune to guest star in an episode of Lucille Ball's second series, *Here's Lucy*. There was a director on the show, but Lucy—the star, series owner, and studio chief—had the final decision on everything. The series regulars were accustomed to Lucy's martinet control, but it was a bit disconcerting for a guest star like me. Who do I listen to? Lucy, or—as I had been taught—the director? Shamelessly, I went with Lucy. Thankfully, she liked everything I did, even taking special time to work with me to make my scenes bigger and better. Needless to say, I never worked for *that* director again. Am I embarrassed? Not really—should I have chosen him over the great Lucille Ball?

With Dean Martin in *Kiss Me, Stupid*

Always smiling, joking, relaxed, and happy on set, Dean Martin was a man of habit: by 11 AM he had a glass in hand, filled with ice and his favorite liquid. He gave the appearance that he never took anything too seriously, and he probably never did, but while on set filming *Kiss Me, Stupid*, Dean never dropped a line of dialogue, missed a mark, rejected a proffered piece of movement or business, or refused another take. He was a thorough professional in every way ... and the most hilarious and spontaneously funny man I've ever met.

With Christine Kaufman and Tony Curtis in *Wild and Wonderful*

Tony carried himself without self-consciousness, projecting an "I'm just an average guy" persona—regardless of the complexity of the role, a "common man" aura that made him a star. On the set of *Wild and Wonderful*, Tony and I discussed his long and star-studded acting career. He mentioned that he was contracted for seven more films. "Seven? That's a lot. Are the roles so great that you couldn't turn them down?" I asked. "They're great paydays," he responded, with a smile and a shrug. Art and Commerce; Tony provided me an early example of those ever-present Twin Deities of acting.

With Raul Julia on the set of *The Penitent*

When film producer Michael Fitzgerald and I were first putting together the financing for *The Penitent*, we were able to get the script to Raul Julia. If he liked the script and agreed to play one of the two leads, the money people, Vista, Inc., agreed to finance the film. We heard from Raul a week later; he believed in the script, but wanted to meet with me first, as I would also be directing.

I flew to San Francisco Airport where I met Raul on a travel layover between assignments. We sat in a coffee shop in Terminal 2 and talked for an hour about the script and his character. Raul agreed to work on the film for one-sixth his usual salary—a testament to the selfless commitment from a lovely man and consummate artist who also had a generous heart.

With Walter Matthau in *The Fortune Cookie*

If you were working in a scene with Walter Matthau, the great danger was to step aside to watch Walter sweep and swirl in one of his brilliant comic character gyrations and forget your responsibility to act your own character. However, when you were up to the task with Walter, his richness of characterization sweetened your imaginative effort.

Larger than life, off-screen as well as on, he was also down-to-earth and generous, graciously co-sponsoring me (with Jack Lemmon) into the Academy of Motion Picture Arts and Sciences.

With Paul Mazursky (cigar) in *World's Greatest Robbery*
(also pictured: R.G. Armstrong and Paul Lambert)

The brilliant, Academy Award® wining writer-director Paul Mazursky began his career as an actor, and I had the pleasure of working with him in two television shows: the *Twilight Zone* and *World's Greatest Robbery*. The latter, a two-hour NBC special event, was one of the final network TV movies shot live and recorded on kinescope.

A couple of years into Paul's successful writing and directing career, he offered me $5,000 (in 1960s money!) for a day's acting in one of his films. All I had to do was be in a tub, nude, at a party scene, and say a few lines. A generous offer; however, the idea of my nude body (I was 340 pounds then) being projected on the big screen was too frightening to consider. I said no.

I never heard from Paul again.

With Bob Newhart in *The Bob Newhart Show*

This episode of *The Bob Newhart Show*, entitled "The Heavyweights," is one of the most enjoyable and best acting experiences of my TV career. Bob was easy to work with, and the writers and director of the show supporting him were superb craftsmen. The other regulars in the cast were welcoming, excellent, and fun people to be around. Bob was living proof that pleasantness, gentle care, and concern have their own rewards, whether in life or a great TV series. Bob's art mimicked his life, off stage and on, and he was what you saw: a brilliant, hilarious, understated, and mischievous gentleman.

With Ray Walston in *Kiss Me, Stupid*

Ray Walston and I sang an unpublished George and Ira Gershwin song in the film *Kiss Me, Stupid*. Ray replaced the original star of the film, Peter Sellers, after his heart attack and inability to return to the set. Unfortunately, Ray and I never quite hit it off, musically or professionally. While acting with Ray, my rhythms were always out of sync and I over-acted, which became obvious in the finished film. Billy Wilder warned me, kindly but impishly at the sneak preview, "Don't buy the new house yet, Cliff." He was, as always, prophetic: the critics morally crucified us.

Years later, Billy joked about my musical efforts in *Kiss Me, Stupid*: "Cliff Osmond. Yes, wonderful, wonderful actor. Unfortunately, he has the musical ear of Van Gogh!"

With (a very young) Jodie Foster in *Gunsmoke*

Jodie began her brilliant acting career at age three; at seven, she was working consistently in television. Recently, a friend told me he had seen an old episode of *Gunsmoke*, featuring both Jodie and me in supporting roles. As I look at that picture now, even through the haze of time, I remember that she was a beautiful child and a practiced, secure performer even then, already knowing how to act properly, cooperatively, and without artifice. I simply love this picture ... a sweet, sweet memory.

Introduction

Why study acting?

Don't.

If you are brilliant and can be assured of maintaining acting brilliance at a desired level of competitive success—for now and for the discernible future—forego study. Return this book quickly to Barnes and Noble, Borders, or Amazon.com and get your money back. Never allow learning to get in the way of achievement. Learning is required only when instinct fails.

Bob Hayes, the Olympic 100-meter dash champion in 1964, was known as "The Fastest Human Alive." He achieved this notable success in spite of the fact he ran wrong. Sprinters of his day were taught to run with toes pointed forward: he ran pigeon-toed. Thank God no one taught him how to run right, although they taught him a few other things, like not running out of his lane and how not to false start—the craft of running, as it were. Mostly, his early coaches just let him run his own way and win world championships at record-breaking times.

If you're the Bob Hayes of acting, don't study. Don't tinker with success. Find the nearest stage or film set; start working. If you're the Fastest Actor Ever, capable of winning every part you audition for, avoid all theories, rules, techniques, and acting exercises: continue doing it your way. I wouldn't even use the word "acting" because it might produce inhibitory self-consciousness.

However, if you have lost more than a few races—failed auditions, a failing career, a non-existent career—you might want to visit the art and craft of acting intellectually and try to figure out what went wrong. Perhaps you will discover a better way of doing it. Heed the words carved in granite above Royce Hall at UCLA: "Education is learning to use the tools which the race has found indispensable."

As a young student actor, I was confronted with such an over-abundance of acting terms, truisms, truths, "should do's" and "you better do's," that I got lost in the forest of information. I became overwhelmed in a thicket of acting insights, bewildered by all the gorgeous leaves of brilliant teaching and learning theories. I yearned for a single organizing set of principles, a simple all-encompassing path through the trees to enable me to move efficiently and unconfused toward my goal of successful acting. I continued my search and found even more brilliant theories, teachers, techniques, principles and methods … and became even more confused how to organize all those elements into one simple, distilled, understandable and clear package.

Simultaneously, serendipitously, and fortunately—but much more ineffectively had I not been so confused—I moved on to a measure of professional success sans organizing principle until, one day, I began to teach.

"Teachers teach in order to learn." After years of acting and teaching, including forty-five years of professional stage and Hollywood TV and film acting, advancing to candidacy for my PhD in Theater History at UCLA, a series of professional TV and film writing assignments, film directing, a stint at story editing on an NBC TV series, writing an acting curriculum used by over forty modeling and acting schools around the country, twenty-five years of individual private acting teaching in Los Angeles, conducting acting seminars and workshops in over a hundred US cities in thirty-four states, 10,000 instructional scenes, and 20,000 students, I finally discovered a single, startlingly fact: good acting is nothing more than what happens in every-day life, only it happens in a special venue ... excitingly.

The ten elements of exciting acting (and life) do not all originate with me ... although I may have given new names to some of them. They have not sprung Minerva-like from my actor's/ teacher's brain. Other acting theorists have dealt with them, in one form or another, since time immemorial, or at least in Western Civilization from the time of the Greeks. They are:

> Making sure a performance is *conflictual*
> Making sure a performance is *real*
> Making sure a performance is *honest*
> Making sure a performance is *interdependent*
> Making sure a performance is *witnessed*
> Making sure a performance is *intense*
> Making sure a performance is *varied*
> Making sure a performance is *complex*
> Making sure a performance is *structured*
> Making sure a performance is *elegant*

Why am I revisiting these elements? The lessons of kindergarten hold: I want to share.

Blessed in a personal forty-five year acting career working intimately with such actors and directors as Jack Lemmon, Shirley MacLaine, Lee Marvin, Armand Assante, Billy Wilder, Stanley Kramer, Raul Julia, Vince Vaughn, Sally Field, Walter Matthau, Lucille Ball, Red Skelton, Robert Ryan, Jim Arness, Carroll O'Connor, George C. Scott, Jody Foster, Kim Novak, Peter Sellers, Dean Martin, Max Von Sydow, and many, many others, I have retained a lingering desire to pass on to others what I discovered from them about acting. This acting book is my paean to these actors, my conduit—from them through me—to other actors, directors, and writers (even to the long-suffering spouses of actors who have to answer that frightening question: "I am good, aren't I, honey? ... Aren't I?"), to lay out a complete, practical and sensible package of acting theory, one that is based on a specific, clear formula for the analyzing, training, understanding, and enjoyment of acting.

Acting is simple: conceptually.

What is difficult—and complex—in acting or any other endeavor, is excellence, so in my teaching I always emphasize the logical simplicity of acting, freeing my students to focus their energies on the more complex task of achieving excellence.

It does not take the IQ of a rocket scientist or neurosurgeon to understand acting, or for that matter, to act well. Some of the finest and most successful actors I have known have had very ordinary IQ's, which is not to denigrate the benefit of intelligence in accomplishing any task: its presence is extremely beneficial.

> *What is primary in acting, however, what the best actors and actresses have in abundance, is the extraordinary courage and insight it takes to live fully and intensely in public: to face, and accept, the deepest truths about oneself and, by extension, of humankind in general, and then be willing to really live out those truths in a real, exciting manner before an audience.*

That is the genius of an actor.

That is the goal of all acting theory, training and practice.

"There is No Such Thing as Acting" is the title of a seminar I conducted a few years ago at a state convention of grammar school through university theater teachers. I chose that title because (1) I hoped its seemingly confrontational tone would attract a large number of attendees to my lecture: it did; (2) I thought it would be challenging and fun to defend myself against 600 extremely intelligent people whose livelihood depended in one way or another on the existence of acting: it was; and (3) I believed that statement to be true.

I still do.

> *Acting is simply a term we use when real emotional life occurs (1) on demand, (2) in front of an audience, (3) with a variety, intensity, pace, and profundity of emotion—and elegance of style— uncommon in the everyday world, and (4) within very narrow, defined parameters of words, movement, and prop-handling.*

Therefore, acting terms and instructions become nothing more than reminders to actors to act, to live on stage, in accordance with these dictates of everyday exciting life.

Consider, for a moment, such acting rules/conditions as "moment-to-moment," "pursue an objective," and "playing against."

"Moment-to-moment" is a command to actors to act a scene without anticipation for what is going to occur next. This acting injunction is nothing more than a real-life term dressed in acting jargon. Moment-to-moment is how we all live, isn't it, perhaps with some vague expectations of future occurrences, but without any definite foreknowledge of the future?

"Pursuing an objective" is another acting concept that states an actor-as-character should have a fundamental goal in the scene.

Once again, the inclusion of an actor's goal in acting is nothing more than a truism of everyday life: purpose is not fundamental to acting alone; all human life is organized around purpose (survival, at its most fundamental level).

The term "playing against" is another suggested performance mode wherein the actor is asked to manifest surface behavior in opposition to inner feelings. Nothing out of the ordinary here, either. Most of us live our everyday lives unacquainted with our deepest feelings: we smile when we're sad; we whistle while we work; we're manic when we're depressed. We invariably veil our inner emotional conditions—whether from ourselves or from others—behind contradictory outer masks. When actors are encouraged by teachers and directors to include these acting elements in their performances, they are simply being asked to live their performance life according to the tenets of everyday exciting life.

Let's say I am invited to a dinner party scheduled to begin promptly at 8 pm. When I arrive, the hostess whispers in my ear, "I want you to sit next to Mrs. Phelps. Talk nicely to her about the ballet and the arts. I don't want to hear a word about your beloved sports. And don't talk in your usual urban accent. Speak articulately, cultured. And no dirty words. This is an elegant party. Be 'up,' fun, not your usual grumpy self. Patricia's going through a divorce. She needs to flirt. Be sexy."

I obey.

I sit next to Mrs. Patricia Phelps, eating the food others have prepared and set before me, using the utensils set on the table by someone else. As instructed, I put away my usual anger and grumpiness and become humorous and sexy. (The role is not difficult; Mrs. Phelps is a deliciously warm and witty woman.)

All evening long, I allow my new real feelings to activate everything I do: my use of language, the way I move my body, my facial reactions, the tone of my voice, the way I handle the wine glass. Mrs. Phelps and I speak happily and sexily, as I was instructed, of the ballet and the arts—no sports—and while speaking of these matters, I sit elegantly upright in the chair to which I was assigned; deftly maneuver the props of the dinner party, the knives, forks and wineglasses. In short, I play the role designated for me that evening.

Am I a good party-goer? A good actor? Or am I a fake, a phony, pretending to be charmed by Mrs. Phelps, pretending with her to feel sexy and fun-loving (instead of my usual grumpiness), pretending to be elegant, holding my knife, fork and wine glass as if I were to the manor born. Even the tux is not mine: I rented it. To be even more honest, I only learned the proper sequencing of fork use this afternoon.

I argue: isn't it I at the dinner party, wearing the tux, eating the food, handling the knife and the wine glass with aplomb? Moreover, isn't it I who speaks about the ballet and the arts, my mouth that forms the words of my instructed limited vocabulary, my voice box that creates the sounds by which my words are heard? Perhaps most importantly, aren't they my emotions, my humor and my sexiness that pass through those words, movements, and gestures to Mrs. Phelps—and with elegance, I might add? Mrs. Phelps is no fool, no party-going neophyte. Had I faked my emotions, my humor and sexiness, she would have immediately caught on. She would have become bored, if not downright offended.

Instead, at one point during the evening, Mrs. Phelps leans over to me and whispers that I make her feel very alive. I smile back and tell her she does the same for me. By the end of dinner, I discover Mrs. Phelps is not an imminent divorcee, but an actress hired by the hostess to get me out of my usual grumpy mode of behavior and into sexiness and fun.

Mrs. Phelps and I both play our roles so well that night that eventually all the other dinner guests stop their dinner conversations and watch us. They find it more entertaining to cease their own direct activity at the dinner table in order to become involved, albeit indirectly, with our lives.

A few of them are so stimulated, in fact, that they invite Mrs. Phelps and me to an even larger dinner party the next week. They want us to enact a long-time married couple: I am to be grumpy and confrontational, to talk politics and sports, to verbally attack a few arrogant friends who need to be put in their places. Mrs. Phelps will play my long-suffering sarcastic wife. They will instruct us on what to say.

Mrs. Phelps and I decide the new parts are right up our emotional alleys and we delightedly agree to attend the next party.

Mrs. Phelps and I are actors, people who have learned to adjust our honest, real, spontaneous behavior to suit the occasion. The script, including the actor's, director's and producer's (party giver's?) interpretation of it, merely designates the parameters of the occasion to be really lived.

Again, nothing new in our acting behavior here: In everyday life, people continually alter their behavior to suit the occasion.

Witness the cold, adversarial lawyer who in trial cruelly cross-examines the witness for the opposing side, and then, a few minutes later, while questioning his own client, suddenly activates his warm, kind, and understanding self. Or the sympathetic minister who almost cries when told by a parishioner the latter has cancer, and then, a few minutes later, goes to the gym and becomes a killer on the handball court. Or the angry, frustrated CEO of a major corporation who works up an enraged fury over a lost contract, then comes home and is tender and loving while reading bedtime stories to her daughter.

All of us, in our everyday lives, work hard to arrange and re-arrange our internal emotional and external behavioral patterns when adapting to new situations, often utilizing dimensions of ourselves rarely known to our friends, colleagues and loved ones. Sometimes we even surprise ourselves with our newly-utilized behavior: "God ... I didn't know that was in me!"

Does that mean we are all actors? Yes. Does that mean we are all excellent actors? No.

What differentiates the everyday actor (all of us) from the pro-fessional actor (a few of us) is the degree to which a person can consistently learn to micro-manage real personal behavior so that it occurs precisely (1) on demand, (2) in front of millions of people, (3) with such uncommon substance and style that it can excite those millions, and (4) within the narrowest proscribed (i.e., scripted) limitations of words and deeds.

That skill, to live a real, honest, exciting and elegant life within such rigid precise parameters, is what is unique, compelling, and difficult about acting ... and why the best professional actors get paid so much and are held in such high regard by their peers and audiences.

Any scene—and the actor's performance within a scene—can be conceptualized, evaluated, and diagnosed—and, when found de-ficient, remedied—by ten essential elements of real, exciting life:

Conflictual, **Real**, **Honest**, **Interdependent**, **Witnessed**, **Intense**, **Varied**, **Complex**, **Structured**, and **Elegant**. Accordingly, this book is organized into these ten subheadings.

These ten elements become the actor's blood pressure test, the temperature reading, the blood analysis, the X-ray, the MRI of acting—and the basis for subsequent correctional guides, nutrition plans, exercise regimens, and pharmacological solutions. The health and wellness of an acting performance are grounded in these ten essential elements of real, exciting life: avoid them at great risk ... to performance and career.

Why only ten? Aren't there thousands, if not millions, of human elements involved in a living performance? Aren't there as many cells in the human body as there are stars in the universe? If acting is real, emotional inner life, how can someone limit the essential elements of acting behavior to only ten?

I have only so many years to live and write this book, and you only have so many rehearsal periods to build a performance and so many years to build a career. Accordingly, we are both impelled to concentrate on the most essential and critical elements in the given task.

Besides, ten is a nice, round number. Our whole numerical system is based on it: ten fingers, ten toes, mathematical exponents to the tenth power, one hundred percent, decathlete, dollars and cents, centimeters, kilograms, megabytes, the Ten Commandments, and all that. Ten is traditional. Ten is magical. Ten is enough. Concentrate and work on these fundamental ten, and you will find, as you work, exponentially, to the tenth, hundredth, thousandth, millionth power (all expansions of ten, by the way), the rest of acting will fall into place.

Part I

The Five Obligatory Elements of Good Acting

There Is No Acting Without Them.

Conflict
Reality
Honesty
Interdependence
Witnessed

Conflict is the foundation of acting;
no foundation, no enduring edifice.

Chapter 1
Making Sure a Performance is Conflictual

Prologue to Conflict

The Ten Essential Elements of Acting, like elements of everyday life, are circular and interdependent: they form a total fabric. Their individual strands flow endlessly, seamlessly, albeit sometimes subterranean, into and out of the other. In order to begin any analysis, we must break that infinite circle at some point, grab a thread, and say: "We start here." Accordingly, I have chosen to start my theoretical analysis of acting with the concept of "conflict."

Other acting analysts might initiate their study of acting with "character," or "emotion," or "practical pointers," and others with "voice and body," "relationships," or "staging." In doing so none of us analyzers is wrong; similarly, none of us is (exclusively) right.

However, all good acting analysts would agree, regardless of the initiating point of departure, the initial thread grabbed as it were, that the elements of acting are, like the elements of life, a total gestalt (a thing greater than the sum of its constituent parts).

Good acting is like Rome, with many roads leading to a common destination: in acting, that destination is a comprehensively-woven fabric of exciting life that moves audiences emotionally and intellectually.

While we initially ask the reader to consider at first each element of good acting separately because that is the way of analysis—isolate a variable, hold "all other things constant"—in the final analysis, the good actor is asked in performance to reweave the total fabric again, to put all ten elements of good acting back together into an uninterrupted, interdependent and living, symbiotic whole.

In choosing to start the theoretical analysis of acting with what a person does, "conflict," (plot), as opposed to any other acting element, such as "character," what a person is—that is, the psychological and emotional aspects underpinning their doing—I am reminded of the old dramatic saw: "Character drives plot; plot reveals character." It could just as easily be said: "Plot reveals character; character drives plot." Who comes first: the chicken or the egg? Is character more seminal to understanding acting behavior, or is plot?

It has been my experience that most actors naturally and initially incline to considerations of character first. A friend of mine, the writer and director Bob Collins, was confronted by an actor on a set who did not "feel like saying a line of dialogue" in a script Bob had written (Bob was also directing). Bob explained to the actor—concerning logical progression of the plot—the importance of delivering the line as written. The actor exclaimed: "But my character would never feel like saying something like that!"

Bob glared for a moment, then replied, "The character I hired you to play would," and walked away.

The dialogue was said—and felt—as Bob had written it. However, the actor's proprietary/territorial point was made: once on set and in production, the actor no longer considered the logical demands of plot to be his primary consideration: his focus was on his feelings, and for most actors feelings—character—trump plot.

Acting is Living

However, being salmon-like by nature, when teaching actors I prefer will-fully to swim upstream to spawn. "Indulge a strength; create a weakness" is my motto. If I were a bodybuilding coach for animals, I would probably demand ostriches to start their strength training with leg lifts and squats, kangaroos with bench presses and pushups. My wife understands my perverseness. In my daily aerobic walk with her, when confronting a steep hill, I attack it. My wife, on the other hand, eases into it. She attacks the downhill.

Consequently, this book starts with emphasis on plot—conflict—over character, emphasizing what I believe are actors' major weaknesses, rather than strengths, on their deficiencies as opposed to abundances, their problems as opposed to preferences, and leave initiating workouts of character to writing teachers who, if sufficiently salmon-like, will take their writing students initially and energetically uphill through the writer's more difficult terrain of character and feelings before moving downhill through a writer's easier and more natural flow of logic and plot.

Conflict: The Name of the Acting Game

The Ancient Greeks are credited with creating conflictual drama in western civilization, and two of their earlier art/ritual traditions contributed to this dramatic development.

One is the ancient Dionysian rites, the passionate ritualistic fertility dances, where rising group passion led to orgiastic fulfillment. Participants in these rites often literally spread seed on the ground, which may seem somewhat unusual—unless one considers the aim of that ancient ritual was to ensure the coming of spring and the promise of new life.

From these Dionysian origins the emotional aspect of acting can be traced.

The other tradition flowing into the development of Greek drama are the elegiac tales told by ancient storytellers at the graves of recently fallen Greek heroes. These storytelling poets used long, mournful, dithyrambic poems, words, verbal logic, instead of bodies, to dance across the emotional landscape, to take passion up from the feet, past the groin and heart, and into the brain and mouth ... and, accordingly, into the logic of conflict and plot. In these public storytelling sessions, they recounted the beginning, middle and end of life and death, of heroes and their heroic engagements. (Homer's *The Iliad* and *The Odyssey* are part of this tradition.)

At some point, the two embryonic traditions co-joined. Choral dancing poured its passionate ecstasies into individual tragic storytelling—thereby organizing emotion into plot. When that happened, early drama took its major leap from ritual dance and graveside storytelling to dramatic modernity.

At some further developmental moment, one or more Greek artists must have decided, *"Why should we just tell the emotional stories of the past? Why don't we go the next step in telling stories about protagonist and antagonist? Why not enact them? Let the heroes live in the present. Let's see and hear both figures in operation. Give us present tense storytelling."*

As a result, actors/storytellers moved out of their dance-like choral and storytelling modes to perform passionate conflictual renderings of past stories in the dramatic present. (The first credited actor to step out of the chorus, to verbally dance the story conflict, as it were, vis-à-vis the chorus, was Thespis. From Thespis comes the word for actor: thespian.)

In this new development of drama and acting, heroic protagonist was now set up onstage versus passionate antagonist. Stories no longer simply talk about hero and villain conflicting: the participants now actually conflict in words and deeds right in front of the audience. (It is interesting to note that—to this day— drama, plays and screenplays are still written in the present tense. Novels, legatees of the older dithyrambic storyteller tradition, are written primarily in the past tense.)

Actors are Conflictors

The basic enactment of conflict in drama is the good guys versus the bad guys, heroes versus villains, cops versus robbers, loan officer versus desperate borrower. Is that a cliché? Perhaps, but that's how clichés get to be clichés: they are truths so well-known that people get bored hearing them.

Actors/characters are the choral antagonists, the emotional contesters of drama. The Ancient Greeks, in particular the great Macedonian philosopher/teacher of the 4th century BCE, Aristotle, called the body of a play or drama the *agon*, or wrestling. Agony in those days did not mean, as it is today, the "agony of defeat." It meant the positive grunting and groaning of both winners and losers, the active energy expended in the attempt to win emotional release.

In the agon of conflictual drama, actors pay physical and emotional prices—emotion can be thought of as inner physical price —to attain victory over the other actor(s).

Drama—in a scene or whole work—thus becomes two or more individuals, or sets of individuals, or, in rare instances, humans versus nature, pitted against one another, set in agonizing opposition, who seek to pin their opponent(s), to force them to the mat, using mind, heart, body, emotions and soul, to emerge victorious. The most apt and cogent definition of drama I know is *character revealed in action*. Character is what character does … in the agonizing pursuit of victory.

(NOTE: Good actors must remember legitimate actor performance energy arises only in real story agony or conflict, out of an actor-as-character's emotional urgency to win. If the actor's energy is sourced in any other manner—for example, an actor's desire to directly affect and "please" an audience, to show the audience what a good actor he is—the acting becomes false and, therefore, off-putting to the audience. While mothers and fathers of such bad actors may be happy their actor-kids are trying so hard, that kind of generalized acting energy—no matter how virtuoso its practitioner—is lesser acting, and it always fails emotionally to engage the largest numbers of audience members. As such, it falls short of its very *raison d'etre*.)

The Three Transcendent Rules of Conflict

There are three overarching rules of on-stage or on-set conflictual acting: (1) You can't hurt someone else physically; (2) You
can't hurt yourself physically; and (3) You can't leave. All else is
permitted; nay, all else is desired.

The first two rules, avoiding physical injury during conflict to
self and/or others, arise from the audience's need to maintain
"aesthetic distance" from the actor to keep the audience one
step removed from *too much* onstage reality.

In good acting, all theatrical facts on stage must lead to engaged
audience feeling, not disengagement. If an audience is confronted with a factually too-real situation with real blood flowing, or,
in the most extreme example, a "snuff movie" in which
someone is really murdered, it becomes terminally, artistically
off-putting. Audiences can take only so much emotional/physic-
al reality before escaping into life-saving shock, which is nothing
more or less than the numbing of the receptors in order to survive emotionally. Aesthetic distance removes the audience from
that shock threshold and is breached by factual excess onstage.

The third rule, the third "no-no" of good acting, occurs when a
character quits in performance, when he ceases to conflict, refuses to really and purposefully listen, see, feel, talk and move toward a goal. (The most egregious form of actor quitting is *fake
acting*. Fake actors never really engage in the first place! They are
too busy "acting.")

To quit in a scene, revealing in words, deeds, or emotions that
"My character gives up here," is to end the scene. When a character's striving in a scene ends, drama ceases. Even if the characters remain onstage, post conflict, as it were, they remain only
funereal presences, their subsequent dialogue and other actions

merely a form of rigor mortis; dead bodies lying in a proscenium box or camera box, subject to legitimate audience burial—yawning.

The brilliant actor, Jack Lemmon, was asked by the host on a late night talk show if he had any advice to young would-be actors. Without hesitating, Jack said: "Tell them they got to be crazy."

The host paused a moment: "You mean the life style; the difficulty getting a role?"

"No," Jack said, "acting itself." He explained, "I do a love story, like *The Apartment*. I meet the girl in Act One; she can't stand me. I spend the rest of the movie trying to get her to love me. In *China Syndrome*, in Act One, I know there's going to be a nuclear meltdown. I spend the rest of the movie trying to convince people to do something about it. I'm telling you, you've got to be crazy to be an actor. You spend your life leaning against the wind, striving after the impossible."

Tactics in Conflict

All written and performed elements in a dramatic scene—including the emotions that invariably arise thereof—are tactics aimed toward achieving simple conflicting goals, or objectives.

An alien comes to earth. He drops into a football stadium and sits among the cheering people. On the grassy ground below are overly dressed-up bulky humans running in all directions, their bodies slamming into other bodies. He is bewildered and confused by the mish-mash of inexplicable activity.

A brown oblong object seems to be the focus of attention. The object is thrown, kicked and carried forward, backward and sideways. People get up, fall down, knock each other down, and gather in groups around the brown object. He asks the man next to him, "What is going on?"

The man answers, "Conflict." The alien blinks. The man adds, "All that activity, all the humans on the playing field, including their handling of the oblong brown thing called a football, and the whistle-blowing men in black and white stripes organizing the activity, is all in the service of goal-seeking. All the activities are tactics seeking a goal. One group of individuals tries to carry the brown ball across the other team's goal more times than the other team carries it across theirs. At core, it's really a very simple game."

That night the alien is invited to the theater He asks the same question: what is happening on stage? He gets the same answer: conflict. All written and performed elements in a dramatic scene —including emotions—are character tactics aimed toward achieving their simple, conflicting goals or objectives.

Objectives: The Core of Conflicts

The clash of conflicting character objectives in a scene is what creates the essential drama. A character's objective in a scene is what a character basically wants in the scene in opposition to what the other character(s) wants. Synonyms for a character's objectives are aims, intentions, purposes, through-lines, main actions, and arcs.

Just as every organ in the human body is formed by evolution to further the human agenda of survival—the heart is designed to pump blood through the lungs (which have extracted oxygen from the environment by breathing), arteries are engineered to carry the now-oxygenated blood to the muscles, the veins are constructed to return de-oxygenated blood to the heart to begin the living process again. In a scene, conflictual actions/tactics (dialogue, voice and logic, large body movement, facial reactions, "prop" handling, and feelings) are all aimed by conflicting characters toward achieving a goal: resolving conflict in each character's respective favor, ending the game with victory.

Tactics are not always direct; they are more often than not indirect, sometimes backtracking, circuitous, lateral, as in football, but they always originate, and are fundamentally meant to operate as—and, most importantly for actors, derive their central energy from—forward-propelling human beings positively engaged in an ongoing struggle to achieve objectives and win.

Resolution

Resolution in drama—or climax—is only realizable if there is a prior conflict occurring. To resolve a situation is to re-*solve* it, to find a more appropriate, more satisfying ending. If there is no conflict, there is nothing to re-solve. More tellingly, from the audience's point of view, if there is nothing to be resolved, there is no point to wait around—to continue listening and looking attentively for two or more hours.

No matter how brilliant an actor may be in portraying life, no matter how profoundly an actor's performance mirrors humanity, the actor's playing of emotion *qua* emotion soon loses its attractiveness. Two hours of emotional release without storytelling—two hours of actors feeling without conflict-seeking-resolution—become a long evening. We are back to Dionysus again, pre-drama, culminating with performers' seeds spreading on the ground, hopefully causing fertilization. While seed-spreading may be fun for the participants, for the rest of us it becomes boringly repetitive, if not downright pornographic to watch. Great drama needs story, passion needs reason, Dionysian ecstasy needs the shaping of Apollo, and emotion needs dramatic conflict and plot.

Conflictual Elements in Good Acting

On stage or on set, dramatic conflict is best realized when two or more characters pursue conflictual objectives in a scene that are (1) *diametrically opposed*, (2) *simply defined*, (3) *all-inclusive*, (4) *active*, (5) *solution seeking*, (6) *unconsciously understood*, and (7) *non-judgmental* (the actor-as-character is unconcerned with the (a) *propriety*, (b) *possibility*, (c) *productivity*, (d) *rationality* or (e) *ultimate success* of their character's objective).

1. Diametric Opposition

Conflictual character objectives should be defined diametrically, 180 degrees apart:

"I want to spend the night at your apartment."
versus
"I want you to go home."

"I want us to get married."
versus
"I want us to stay single."

"I want to pay as little as possible for this coat."
versus
"I want you to pay as much as possible."

If the conflictual opposition between two characters is less than 180 degrees, tension is automatically reduced (and reduced tension leads to reduced audience engagement emotion).

Press your middle fingers of each hand hard against one other, in opposition. Maximum tension is created when the fingers of both hands are exactly opposite, forming a straight line across the two opposing hands, fingers pushing directly against one another. Tension lessens when the hands and fingers—objectives—become less than diametrically opposed, culminating in no tension when the hands or fingers are identical or overlapping.

Anything less than 180-degree opposition between character objectives lessens the emotional and dramatic possibilities in the scene.

2. Simply Defined

Character objectives in a scene should be simply defined. Actors should avoid complex "psychobabble" when defining the objectives in a scene. They should refrain from stating a character's objective in convoluted terms. For example:

> *"I want to rectify the betrayals of my past because my father left home when I was six ...."*

Or...

> *"I want to prove to my wife that I am a competent male provider because she comes from a bourgeois Republican family and her Neanderthal father ...."*

Or...

> *"I want the psychological and sensual understanding that my husband doesn't give me and that my father gave me when I was a young girl when I used to sit so contentedly on his knee, and that's why I am sitting on yours."*

All of the above psychoanalytic viewpoints and their emotional/psychological case histories may be both true and important motivational and factual conditions driving the objectives of the plot, but the character goals—the core concept in motivation being the word motive—reason for being—are simple. The better statements of objectives in the above examples are:

"I want to marry you"
(in order to solve my feelings of betrayal).

"I want a job promotion"
(in order to provide more money for my husband).

"I want to have sex with you"
(in order to survive the sensual barrenness of my marriage and to re-experience the love my father gave me).

Good scenes, when they are played by good actors, originate in direct, simple, declarative statements of *"what* the character wants," as opposed to *"why* the character may want it. "Why" has to do with character motivation, with the emotional origins of actions, which are generally infinitely more complex, but should never be viewed as a statement of the character's objective itself.

Characters are emotionally complex people seeking simple tactical solutions—straightforward objectives—to make their lives emotionally uncomplicated.

3. Fundamental

An actor often will say to me, "I see three objectives in the scene."

I say, "No. There is only one."

They invariably retort: "In the first third of the scene, the character's objective is…."

I say: "No. Stop. There is only one objective in a scene. There may be several mini-actions, sub-objectives, changing tactics, but they all spring from and contribute to the one fundamental objective."

Trees have many branches; in fact, some trees have branches so large they seem trunks unto themselves. However, just as a tree can only have one basic trunk, a character in a scene can have only one basic objective. The same holds for a whole play or film: there is only one overriding main objective or "character arc" in the whole piece, one trunk, holding perhaps armfuls of branches.

I reiterate: "In any scene, play or film, there is only one overall objective."

4. Active

Character objectives in a scene are always active. On a film set, note the director yells "Action!" to start the scene. The director does not yell "Feel!'" or "Show me the problem!" or "Emote!" The director yells "Action," he wants the actor to do something!

In good acting, the word "acting" is a dynamic operational verb; it is not a noun, not a static definition. Acting theorists as far back as Aristotle cautioned actors on just that fact, that acting means "to do." Moreover, note the suffix -*ing* is at the end of the verb, acting. As such, acting is more than simple present tense: it is present participle. It is act-*ing*, do-*ing*.

Good acting is, therefore, always a state of becoming, not one simply of being. The pursuit of a character's objective is ongoing, still operational throughout the scene, always alive in a most present-tense dynamic state.

Consider the simplest of human activities, even the seemingly inactive, unconscious "tics of behavior" that characters/people exhibit in a scene/life, such as fidgeting with a collar, or clicking on and off a ball point pen, or brushing the hair off the neck and from behind the ears.

One may think of the activities and actors playing these activities as static, inert revealers of character; nouns, emotional conditions, rather than action verbs. However, tics at their core, although revealing of character, have their origin in actively pursuing objectives. They are ways in which a person actively attempts to rein in and circumscribe inner emotions that threaten to spin them out of control and create unproductive outer behavior. The intent is to enable people to constrain excessive emotion in order to focus more economically on their essential goals. They are—like any human action—only secondarily and inadvertently revealing of a character's emotion.

Unconsciously, the "tic-ing" person is saying to himself, "If I can overcome my nervousness by soothingly playing with my hair, or by releasing unwanted energy by the clicking of a pen, or by hiding my nervousness with the fidgeting of a collar, I may be better able to focus my emotional energies to achieve my goal vis-à-vis the other person."

Alternatively, have you ever viewed a catatonic? They are the height of passivity, right? Then why do catatonics seem so dramatically mesmerizing, so filled with attractive energy? Because catatonics are actively trying to keep all stimuli out of their life, actively attempting to push away all sensory seductions bombarding them from what they see as an unfriendly world.

The same phenomenon occurs when sitting at a bar or on a plane and trying to avoid a person intent on engaging you in conversation. It takes an inordinate amount of active energy to get the other person to cease his friendly overtures, to convince him with your back, your indifference, and your silence to stop talking! That's what makes being at a dull party or a friendly drunken bar so enervating: it is physically exhausting to keep unwanted people at a distance.

Even reviewing the past is active! Characters look back only to move forward. They seek in the reservoir of their personal history active solutions to deal better with the present. As George Santayana said, "Those who cannot remember the past are condemned to repeat it." Characters actively (and energetically) pull back a bow of the past to shoot the arrow of the present more tellingly into the future.

All human activity is active.

Passive Statements

Actors often make a mistake in defining a character's objective in the passive voice. The misguided actor says:

"My character doesn't want to be here."

"My character doesn't want to get hurt."

"My character doesn't want to go with him."

My first response to such statements is, "Then what does he want to do? There must be an active reason they are in the scene in the first place."

Passive statements are problem avoiding, not problem confronting; tension averting, rather than tension producing. The passive voice (in defining objectives) creates inertia, not drama; lethargy, not energy; implosion, not explosion.

Another actor in a scene will similarly say to me, "My character wants to leave."

I invariably raise my eyebrows once again. "Then why doesn't he just leave right off the bat? Why does he keep talking in the scene for five more pages? If all he wants to do is to leave, why doesn't he just walk out of the scene?"

Obviously, the character is trying to achieve something positive and active by staying on stage and talking so much. After all, it takes energy to talk for five pages: it must arise out of some purpose.

A character who hangs around talking for five pages—even when and if he says during the scene he wants to leave—is invariably passively-*aggressively* trying to stop the other person from making, cajoling, begging him to stay.

Elongated talk (such as the example above) seeks eventually to reduce the costs of leave-taking by convincing the other character of the logic of the break up, convincing her that it is "for the best." If the departure-desiring character is successful in getting the other character to acquiescence to the logic of the parting, he can minimize the guilt and reduce the emotional cost of leave-taking.

Therefore, a better and more active way to state these seemingly passive objectives is:

> *"My character is trying to **stop** the other character from wanting to be with me."*

> *"My character is trying to **stop** the other character from hurting me."*

*"My character is trying to **stop** the other character from pursuing me."*

Stopping someone is doing something active. It underscores the aggressive intent in passive-aggressive behavior, and it is almost always a more interesting and energizing acting choice.

Whining

When an actor-as-character stands around in a scene—whining, moaning, and complaining—but not actively trying to change the seemingly-problematic circumstances, the audience begins to distrust the severity of the complained pain. "Look; if it's that bad, you would do something about it: move out, quit your job, or find another boyfriend." Whining, moaning, and complaining are off-putting to an audience because the whiner is in actuality pretending it hurts more than it does.

A student, both a colleague and a friend of mine, Carlos Alazraqui, coined the term "loser's laments" for the sounds of whining, moaning, and complaining, as well as its cousin sound, frustration. Those attitudes/sounds emanate from people who have accepted the inevitability of losing, who have accepted defeat in the scene before it begins. Only guilt and the good offices of their competitor remain in the complainer's need for victory. Whiners seek victory through mercy.

A good rule of acting: *"Don't whine; win! Don't complain; convince! Don't suffer; solve!"* Actors who obey these injunctions are invariably much more appealing and interesting to watch.

5. Forward Looking

A good acting performance is forward-looking.

An acting teacher, writer, professor, and former college mate, Robert Cohen, in one of his many wonderful, instructive books on acting, offers an illustration of the forward-looking, solution-seeking nature of good acting. On a page he draws a tri-part diagram: on the right side is an outhouse, in the center is a man running left-to-right, on left is a bear, running left-to-right as well.

Robert states that if you ask actors to describe the picture, most will say, "A bear is chasing a man" or "The man is running from the bear." Robert offers a better acting analysis: the man is positively, purposely, actively *running to the outhouse*. The outhouse is the solution to his problem. If the man can get to the outhouse, the problem of the bear is solved. (Whether the man gets there or not, whether the outhouse is a logical, productive, or even realizable objective, are concerns to be addressed by the scene's unfolding, but not by the character's initial choice of objective.)

6. Unconsciously Understood

In preparation and rehearsal, the good actor looks down on the script from on high, defines his objective in the scene, but then must come down to earth again when enacting the character. In performance, the actor must subsume his knowledge of the character's objective to the level of consciousness appropriate to the character's everyday human behavior.

Good actors are hired to play human beings, and most human beings have little awareness of their overall objectives in life. They tend to live moment-to-moment, with little conscious discernment of the inner aim or purpose propelling their everyday activities, unaware of the purposeful method in their operational madness.

For example, in a scene a man wants a divorce. That is his fundamental objective, however, when he enters the house, he is unaware of his ultimate intent. He enters (he thinks) with the goal of coming home, eating dinner, and uninterruptedly watching the TV movie, or, more likely, sports. Within five minutes—much to his surprise—he and his wife are fighting about what to eat, what TV show to watch … until, finally, at the end of the scene, he screams at her that he wants a divorce. Only then does his true intent—the reason behind all his negative actions in the scene—become part of his consciousness.

The dissenting actor may ask: how is it possible for an actor to consciously discover during scene analysis what is going on throughout the scene—that is, in preparation, defining the fundamental objective of the scene—and, in the next moment, during performance, subsume it down into the character's unconscious?

My answer: We humans do it every day.

I go upstairs intending to get my wallet. I turn the corner to my room. I walk over to the dresser. I reach into the drawer. By now I no longer am consciously aware of my original intent. (No age jokes, please.) While thinking of something else, I still pick up my wallet, even though I have became totally unconscious of the reason for which I came upstairs. Conscious awareness of my initial goal has receded deep into my muscle memory, disappeared into the sub-cognitive portion of my brain, but my commitment to my objective remains—and guides my exertions—beneath any level of conscious awareness.

After picking up my wallet, I head downstairs to go the store. I get into the car. I pull out of the garage. I turn left at the corner, chattering away to the person next to me. I become—and remain—consciously unaware of where I am going, yet I continue on the path to—and subsequently arrive at—the store.

Cognition is not a necessary condition for a human's active goal-seeking. The ability of the actor initially in scene preparation to analyze and commit to an objective and then forget his objective in performance—to become unconsciously unaware after he has once been consciously aware, to renew innocence after a period of illumination, to act stupidly after having attained intelligence —is a natively human talent.

A good actor develops it to a high art.

7. Non-Judgmental

Once again, drama reflects everyday life. People strive mightily in everyday life for objectives that are improper, impossible, unproductive, illogical, or ultimately destined for failure. Therefore, in defining a character's objective in a scene, the actor must eschew personal judgment vis-à-vis the character's goals, and should not define the character's goals or objectives in terms that are, for the actor, (a) *proper*, (b) *possible*, (c) *productive*, (d) *rational*, and (e) *successful*.

Consequently, the good actor must often grant his characters the right to pursue those impossible, unproductive, unreasonable, and unrealizable goals, with all the verve and energy, innocence, and, perhaps, stupidity, that many people comically or tragically pursue them in everyday life.

Some humans commit suicide to punish lovers who are already dead. Some people bite the hands that feed them, while knowing they will starve to death in consequence. Some people take out a mortgage they know they can never repay. Their irrational character goals are the very stuff of comedy and tragedy.

Judgments, therefore, on whether a character's goal has or has not propriety, possibility, productivity, logic, and inevitable success are not judgments, in fact, for the actor to make, but for the audience to make *ex post facto* when the drama is over.

Actors must trust that audiences are well able mentally to chew and digest their own dramatic food during and after performance. They do not need the actor to predigest the performance and spit it out in judgmental bites, to judge the character's objective in advance of the conclusion, to generate pabulum in performance, and then patronizingly spoon-feed it to the audience.

7a. Propriety

Political correctness is a political posture, not an artistic one: a personal soap box is too small a stage to enact a valid performance.

> *An actor-as-character should commit only to the character's political, social, and religious agenda, not the actor's.*

A character's objective may or may not be in conformance with the actor's personal value system or even society's everyday norms, but the actor must remember that he is hired to play the actor-as-character-in-performance self, not the actor's everyday self.

Actors and audience have a contract. The audience agrees when entering the theater to leave their usual societal judgments at the door and grants the actor the same freedom. In performance, the actor is granted permission to explore the full range of human behavior possibilities in the drama, within the script's demands and without consideration of everyday extra-theatrical propriety.

This *laissez-faire* compact between actor and audience frees the actor to operate as a scientist in a lab, contractually obligated only to create, collect, and present the unbiased data of a character's life.

If the actor takes moral exception to the character he has been hired to play, he should refuse the employment contract. Once the actor accepts the role, however, he must confine his sense of propriety to the logic of the play and character.

One of the great joys of acting is the artistic freedom to operate immorally, unethically, or improperly if the character so requires.

I once had an accomplished student who rejected a script I had given him to perform in class because he said its tone, language, and content flew in the face of his religious beliefs. I immediately exchanged that script for a more acceptable one. After class, I asked him if, as a fundamental Christian, he ever stood up in church to bear witness to his sins: the lust, the envy and the anger in his heart.

He said he did.

I said that is exactly what actors do. They bear witness to the wide-ranging condition of the human heart so the audience—their parish—can learn from it.

For the good actor, if the script so designates, the violent character has a legitimate reason to kill, the thief character to steal, and the whore character to make a living. Good acting is the emotional "hooking up" with a character's moral system without the usual everyday societal judgment being applied. All an audience asks from an actor in performance is "More!" The audience reserves its moral and ethical judgment on the script and the character for later, on the drive home; the actor-as-character, however, is judged only on creative or aesthetic considerations.

7b. Possibility

The possibility—or even likelihood—of achieving a character's goal should never be a determining factor in an actor defining a character's scripted objective.

Consider: many goals are impossible to attain in everyday life, but many of us desperately seek them nonetheless. As long as the character believes that the goal is possible, any objective consistent with the logic of the script is dramatically viable for the actor to choose.

I am reminded of the death of a loved one in everyday life. Grief counselors often say that by accepting someone's death, sadness abates and "closure" occurs. This implies that during sadness, during pre-closure, as it were, emotion maintains because the mourner has not yet accepted the loved one's death. The grieving mourner remains sad because he still wants the dead person back again. An impossible goal? Yes. Does that stop usually rational humans from wanting dead loved ones back for a day, a month, a year, or forever? No.

7c. Productivity

Some objectives in life are not necessarily good or beneficial for us, yet people strive mightily for them nonetheless. Good actors do the same. Eventual productivity has nothing to do with a character's choice of a goal during the scene or the tenacious commitment to that objective. Characters fight as valiantly for counter-productive goals as much as they fight for productive goals.

For example: in most love situations, one of the lovers always seems to be striving more than the other to avoid a long-term commitment (no exclusivity, no engagement, no marriage); yet, at the end of the script, if the two characters achieve a permanent "happy ending," the initially resistant character's objective was for him an unproductive goal. Nonetheless, that didn't stop that person from pursuing it wholeheartedly prior to— *thank God*—the happy ending.

(NOTE: Happy endings occur when characters want productive goals and win, or want counterproductive goals and lose. Sad endings occur when characters want unproductive goals and win, or strive for counterproductive goals and—unfortunately for them—achieve them.)

Ultimate productivity or non-productivity of a character's goal is an irrelevant consideration in the actor-as-character's initial selection of their objective.

7d. Rationality

Dramatic and comedic characters almost always, by definition, make mistakes in selections of objectives and actions; certainly much more often than they make correct choices. Consider: if characters were always rational, straight-thinking and logical, they wouldn't be in comedy and tragedy in the first place!

Was Don Quixote rational in tilting with windmills? Was Prometheus rational in thinking he could get away with stealing fire from the gods? Was Hamlet rational in following a ghost's demands? If a character makes only rational choices in a film or play, the actor's performance would last two minutes, instead of two hours.

Mental and emotional blind alleys are the geography of comedy and drama. No one wants to pay $100 a ticket on Broadway to watch highly rational people perform highly rational, intelligent, sanitized action for two hours. We soon grow bored with them and their choices, as we often do in everyday life. In fact, we go to the theater to escape those *reasonable people* (us); we go to the theater to watch, enjoy, and learn from characters' irrational mistakes.

7e. Success

A major mistake that actors make in defining an objective in any scene is "end gaming" the script, choosing the character's objective in accordance with what the character achieves at the end of the scene. Sounds like cheating, doesn't it? It is. It's like sneaking a peek at the Christmas presents and then acting surprised when they are opened Christmas morning.

Such actors' foreknowledge becomes emotional armor for the actor; that is, the actor wants to protect themselves in performance from the emotional shocks of surprises, discoveries, reversals of fortune that can occur when they, in a real performance, unknowingly move toward climax of the scene. To preclude this, the actor-as-character decides in advance to know when the spouse is going to leave or when the mother is going to die so they avoid the emotional shocks that unanticipated scene-life might cause. (Would that the actor had that ability in everyday life!)

A second reason for actor foreknowledge is that the actor wants the audience to think their character is analytically smart: "My character knew all the time what was going to happen. My character is an appealingly bright, all-knowing, and all-wise character." Or, the actor wants the audience to know how bright they are: "Aren't I a bright, all-knowing actor, figuring everything out like this in advance?"

End-gaming a scene—playing the beginning of a scene with emotional/intellectual knowledge of the end—is false acting, usually the sign of an intellectually bereft and emotionally insecure actor who does not trust his ability to portray real human events and emotions … life.

Difficulty with Objectives

The analysis of scene objectives is often the single most difficult aspect of an actor's analytical craft to refine.

Actors, like most people, are often taught early in life to cover up their tactical "method" in their operational "madness," to steer clear of admitting freely, candidly, honestly what motivates them in their everyday doing and saying. They are taught at an early age to avoid admitting the self-servingness in their actions: self-servingness is bad; it is selfish.

Therefore, to make it easier for actors to develop more cogent insight into purposes, needs and goals, allow me to lift the burdensome societally-inflicted shame of "selfishness" off actors' backs by drawing this distinction between self-servingness and selfishness: self-servingness should only be considered selfish when it benefits me exclusively. When it benefits others as well as me—and when the cost is primarily to me and not to others—then I can be considered to operate at the height of unselfishness.

Think of the paragon of Western unselfishness: Jesus. Jesus may have chosen to die on the cross, but his mother certainly didn't want him to hang to his death. His friends, including Mary Magdalene and the disciples—minus Judas, of course—would certainly have preferred him alive for a few more years, but Jesus (selfishly? unselfishly?) ascended the cross to die. He considered it his destiny. His self-servingness in ascending the cross benefited others, as well as himself, and came at such a high cost to himself that we call it unselfish. In fact, we consider the act sacrificial, noble, sublime, heroic, and even divine. (Had it benefited only him, we would have called it the height of selfishness to choose to die like that in front of his mother and friends.)

Self-servingness and objective-seeking are the essence of all human life and cannot be avoided. It is beyond judgment and choice. A character in performance who operates without self-servingness—an objective—is lifeless and false because it is false to the material logic of life.

As an antidote to an actor's unproductive tendency to goal-obfuscation—and as a means to exercise to strengthen the actor's ability to search for the objective truth in any scene—I recommend that all actors spend the rest of their lives looking honestly and courageously at the objectives of their own everyday life. (NOTE: Life is a very cheap textbook; prepaid.)

My contention is that, because all knowledge proceeds from self-knowledge, actors will never understand a character's objectives in a scene until they understand their own in everyday life. Three times every day, the actor should ponder a recently completed event in their life, and ask: "What did I fundamentally want from that other person? What basic purpose made me do what I did? What was the intention behind my action? What aim did I have that made me feel good or bad when I did or did not achieve it?"

The process will not be easy at first. Answering objective-defining questions honestly requires a difficult escape from a limiting and learned state of self-judgment. It requires tenacity and courage to uncover and, frankly, face the truth of our daily goal-seeking, to hack vigorously through all the foliage of surface obfuscations and rationalizations that our mind creates to uphold our self-favorable view and honestly confront ourselves.

I assert that no actor can easily learn to define character objectives and scene conflict without a deep, educated understanding of their own operational life objectives.

Summary: Conflict

"There is a conflict in each and every scene?"
"Yes."

"In each and every—"
"Yes."

"Each—"
"Yes."

"Every...?"
(My silence)

"What about a love story?"
"What about a love story?"

"Don't both people want the same thing in a love story? Where is the conflict in that? There must be scenes, especially in love stories, that involve an exception to the conflict requirement."

My lifelong experience with love—you check it out against yours—informs me that each partner in a love relationship is always trying to convince the other partner to conduct their wonderful loving relationship **on their terms.** *Love is an inevitable and ongoing battle between what one of two partners in a loving relationship sees as the best way to maintain the loving relationship and what the other loving partner sees as the alternative best way to maintain the loving relationship. In pop psychology, Mars versus Venus; lovers constantly struggle with opposing views. Love, therefore, becomes a fervently-desired, energetically-sought, well-intentioned oppositional attempt by two people to join together "on my terms." There is always conflict in that.*

Consider your typical "character play," where two characters seem to sit around and talk endlessly with one another for an entire play: no one screams or stands up and hurls bricks or swings bats at the other. The script often simply involves two friends and coworkers sitting on a porch and dis-

cussing the inner workings of the office; or perhaps two old men having lunch the last Friday in every month in Central Park and discussing their lives; or two sisters sitting on a swing in the front yard and discussing their entire sibling past. Where is the conflict in any of that?

Read the play carefully and you will invariably find two characters coming at each other from two different philosophical stances. They almost always have contrasting and conflicting personalities (and, therefore, different emotional needs), and invariably exhibit the critical need to get the other to agree with their world view … so much so that they are willing to spend a month, a year, or a lifetime talking, talking, talking, convincing, convincing, convincing, and trying, trying, trying to get their opponent to accede to their world vision, which may or may not be anything more than who deserves the one available key to the executive bathroom, which of the two old men a now long-dead girlfriend really loved, or who was Mama's favorite?

Many years ago, I was fortunate to have dinner with the wonderful dancer and choreographer, Alwin Nikoli. He was a gentle, disarmingly kind man, filled with sweet creative intelligence, and he listened patiently as I burst forth with youthful enthusiastic comments about theater … until I said, "Drama is conflict."

He suddenly lost all patience and glared at me. "Nonsense," he said. He rose from his seat and started toward the bathroom. "Nonsense." While he was gone, dessert was served, but I had difficulty swallowing my chocolate cake. I was miserable because I had made Mr. Nikoli angry.

Before he returned, the mutual friend who had organized the dinner party tried to explain to me Mr. Nikoli's behavior. "Mr. Nikoli has seen enough personal ego conflict in the Broadway dance and theater to last a lifetime, and didn't even want to consider the concept, in any form. That's why his choreography is always predominantly light, airy, and humorously puckish," she concluded.

Upon his return from the bathroom, Mr. Nikoli became as sweet and charming as ever. He and I talked of many things, but I never again spoke of conflict. However, at one point in our conversation, I thought (but I was smart enough not to say). "Doesn't the beauty and fascination with choreography itself involve putting dancers in conflict with gravity and the limitations of the human form?"

Truth begets truth. If the actor wants the
audience to believe, the actor has to believe.

Chapter 2
Making Sure a Performance is Real

A. The Necessity for Reality in Good Acting

If conflict is the name of the game in acting, reality is its first rule. James Cagney, an American film actor from the 1930s through the 1960s, once defined acting: "I guess if I want the audience to believe, I've got to believe."

Good reality acting flows from the actor's personal and real emotional involvement in what is going on onstage. Good reality acting is not fake acting. It is not "make believe" (except in the sense of making the audiences believe).

Good acting is not just about life: it is life.

No substitutes are allowed in the conflictual game of acting: the actor really plays the game. Once you agree to play the game of acting, you, the actor-as-character, will literally engage in the conflict. You, the actor, will really take the emotional hits. You, the actor, will really sustain the effort. You, the actor—your actual person—will now be the living character.

Does that mean I will play me in every scene? The actor-as-character in every scene will always be me? Yes. Why else would I hire you? I send you the check, I want the whole you: the outer and the inner you.

Beginning actors often say, "I like to act because I can pretend to be somebody else." My reaction is always the same: being somebody else defies physical law. You may be a different aspect of yourself, a newly reconfigured aspect of your personality, but the same molecules are always still involved in performance.

Actors may change behavioral form from character to character, but they are still themselves. Actors in performance are emotional Gumbys capable of twisting themselves to-and-fro, into any emotional shape the script requires."What side of me do you want tonight?" is the proper question the actor asks himself when reading a new script. To play a character is to emphasize one aspect of your personality over another. "Do you want me to be the hateful side of me tonight; the gentle side; the confused side?"

Sometimes the demands of a role may so antithetical to the actor's everyday operating mode that in performance our friends and lovers may not recognize us. They say: "That is not him or her." What surprises them is that they have never seen us behave in that manner before. They can finally know the truth of our good acting performance: it is us.

However, if an actor wishes to continue to deny a particular revealed side of herself, she always has the cover of "character," as in, "That was just the character, sweetheart; not me."

I remember a student actress who had a torrid love scene to play with a very handsome young man in class. Her husband paid a surprise visit the day we filmed that scene. After the scene was over, I apologized to him for having his wife play a love scene on his first visit to class.

He smiled and said he was "cool" with the scene. "I know she was just playing a character."

"Right," his wife said, and she winked to me on the way out.

Lie to your spouse, lie to yourself, but never lie in front of the audience.

Shakespeare's Hamlet gives the following advice to the traveling Players:

> *"...suit the action to the word, the word to the action; with this special observance, that you o'erstep not the modesty of nature; for any thing so overdone is from the purpose of playing, whose end, both at the first and now, was and is, to hold, as t'were, the mirror up to nature; to show virtue her own feature, scorn her own image, and the very age and body of the time his form and pressure."*

> *Hamlet,* Act III, Scene ii

Real acting demands that the acting that happens onstage or on-screen is consistent with everyday life as the audience knows it: Shakespeare's "mirror up to nature." All acting patterns and performance choices must be measured ... without exception ... against that ever-guiding ruler of acting: the mirror of real emotional life.

"Real emotional life" does not mean that all activity on stage must be "naturalism," conforming in physical detail to photographic reality. In fact, the actor's outer form on stage or on set may be abstract, surreal, phantasmagorical ... but the life of the actor inhabiting and living amidst those unnatural forms must be real. Performance life must be driven and inhabited by human emotional reality.

Does that mean, literally, everything that happens on stage or on set must be consistent and logical to a human being's everyday emotional behavioral life?

Yes.

How can real emotional life be fully and legitimately attained on a stage or a movie set? Isn't that too harsh a standard, too un-realistic, too impossible a condition for the actor to achieve?

No.

While admitting that achieving performance reality consistent with everyday emotional life is often very difficult for beginning, and some advanced actors, to understand, appreciate, and achieve—and, while it is one of the most critical, controversial, misunderstood, and misapplied arenas of acting theory, training, and practice—it is the singular most necessary concept to under-stand, accept, and execute if the actor wants to fulfill his fidu-ciary trust to the audience.

Everything else can be false on a stage or film set, but never the emotional life of the actor.

Why do so many people, including many actors, believe acting is false, fake, pretend (in the sense of not real), make-believe, a physical mimicking of life forms, rather than an actual living of it?

Most people base their ideas about acting on secondhand in-formation too often gleaned from people who have never seen or done excellent acting. Or, they derive information from excellent actors who act extremely well, but don't really understand why.

Surprisingly, many successful actors lack a firm understanding of what excellent acting is. They often know what works for them, but they have no synthesized body of theory outside their successful practice to pass on. Frequently they are as guilty as newcomers in promulgating misinformation to outsiders.

Another possible reason that acting-as-real-life is misinterpreted is that a majority of people (actors and non-actors alike) simply find it hard to believe, on stage or off, that any human being (in this case, an actor) can have such tremendous control over her human instrument and that she can alter real behavior to suit the occasion, and be able to do all this on a moment's notice. It is inconceivable to skeptics that anyone could mold their personal behavior with such precision and consistency over such a wide range of scripted possibilities.

The Actor's Purpose Relative to the Audience

The requirement to be emotionally real in performance does not arise from some infallible proclamation of the God of Acting. Rather, it arises from the actor's fundamental practical purpose to move an audience to the discovery of themselves.

I often ask beginning students, "Why do you go see a play or film? If we can understand the audience's purpose in attending an acting performance—perhaps it will help us discover how best to act in the manner to achieve that audience's purpose." I remind them that the audience who pays the piper calls the actors' tune.

The most common response I get from students is: "I go to the theater and movies to escape or to be entertained."

I ask them a follow up question: "What are you escaping from?"

They generally answer, "The boredom of my everyday life."

When I ask about the goal of seeking "entertainment," they give a response close to the dictionary definition of the word: they seek "distraction, amusement" from their everyday lives. (The French word from which the English word "entertainment" is derived is *entrainment*, which means to "carry along, bring with you.")

Most humankind lives a muted existence; in the words of the great playwright, Arthur Miller, in *View from the Bridge*, "... now we settle for half; and so it must be." Consciously or unconsciously, humans realize unrestrained passion, emotion, is personally expensive. Passion's heat, operating without surcease, if lived un-cooled for too long a period of time, can be all-consuming.

A long, sane life dictates emotional economy, so, in order for humans to survive for an extended period of time, life requires we put away some of our passion to conserve our energy, protect it, and resist passion's daily seductive pull. We save some passion for a rainy day.

However, the economical practice sometimes leads to the following conundrum: we wake up on that rainy day and look for our passion, but discover that we have put it so far away we're not even sure where it is anymore. Sometimes—and this occurs especially after a truly extended period of non-use—we reach a point where we're not even sure we ever had it. "Am I still capable of feeling love, hate, and sexual excitement? I think I remember feeling those things once, when I was young; before I was married; before my work as a lawyer; before my father died a violent death … before … before … before; but I'm no longer sure."

Actors' performances provide an opportunity, a seductive pull and urgency, to rediscover, to reactivate, and to renew our lost, muted, hidden-away selves, as well as our dulled passions. No one is, by the way, intrinsically a dull person; everyone has the capacity, the potential, for deep feelings. Dull people have simply dulled themselves emotionally to survive. They are self-anesthetized.

A question arises: why don't audiences simply stay at home or go to a friend's living room to have their escaping, entertaining, passionate experiences in the relative comfort and cheapness of their own personal environment. "Tonight, at 8 PM, I'll sit in the bedroom alone—or with my friends—and have a good cry," or "On Saturday, at 3 PM, I'll go to the local meeting hall with my friends and have a good laugh."

We can't. We audiences need a mediator, an interlocutor, someone transformational placed between deep emotional experience and ourselves. That interlocutor, the guide across our personal River Styx, who takes us from the region of our dulledness to our inner excitement, is the actor in performance. Actors are emotional craftsmen who, through their work, enable audiences to achieve what they can't achieve on their own: a desired heightened emotional state within a safe, predictable environment.

The Script versus Performance

Audiences come to a theater to watch actors act. All other activities in the theater or on a film set are supportive of the centrality of actors in the theatrical experience.

Producers secure the financing necessary to produce the recorded life of the actor. Writers are hired to create a story so actors can live within a plotted context. Dialogue is written to give actors something that is emotionally revealing to say. Directors are hired to create a physical and visual context within which the actor lives. Lighting is created to enable the actor to be seen well. The sound department is hired so the actor can be heard. Film and video stock visually records the lives of the actors. And so it goes.

Theater and film originate with, focus on, and revolve around the actor's central participation in the theatrical process. Story may be the vehicle, but actors' acting is the *raison d'etre*, the driver, the engine of theater and film experience. If the story were the critical element in drawing an audience to the theater, audiences could simply buy the script in the bookstore or go online and read it.

Audiences come to the theater willing to be moved, eager to be moved, but they need a catalyst to overcome their unconscious threshold of emotional reluctance that keeps them from self-organizing in the first place into an auto-stimulating emotional experience.

During the theatrical transformational process, the audience enters the theater to see a play or film. They know a piece of written material has already been preconceived, predetermined. They know that the characters onstage are actors playing their parts. They know that the upcoming events have been preordained, rehearsed; the conclusion is preset. They also know the context is a false reality. The set of a living room has been built of often prefabricated, insubstantial material; the two-dimensional walls are illuminated not by the sun, but with theatrical lighting.

The lights dim, the curtain rises—and this is the moment of theatrical transformation, the creative alchemy, made possible by the audience's willingness to suspend incredulity: EMOTIONAL REALITY occurs. The audience's inhibiting reluctance is overcome, transmuted by the emotional reality of the actors' performances. In spite of the audience's prior reluctance—the reason they couldn't have the emotional experience on their own, why they have spent all that money to go to the theater—the final "click" occurs. The reality of actors in living performances transports the audience to a state that has been called by Coleridge, "the willing suspension of disbelief."

"My God, I know it's a play or a film," the audience says. "They are only actors. I know the actors are going to speak previously written dialogue. I know the conclusion of the story before it starts because I read the review … but … but … it's really happening."

The actor believes; the audience believes. The actor feels; the audience feels. Fiction is translated into fact. Emotional truth is created and shared. The audience has rediscovered its passion.

Kinesthesia

How does an actor's emotional performance transfer to the audience? What is the actual physical process by which an audience's repressed passion is activated?

Perhaps there is some molecular tangible entity, or concoction of entities, that, when activated within the actor in performance, is released and travels through the air with targeted precision, picking out audience members one-by-one in a darkened theater, at random, and/or with precise aim, or for some other reason?

Cliff Osmond

The process by which emotional experience is transferred from actor to audience is called kinesthesia.

The operational dynamic is this: First, the actor is stimulated by performance events to feel. Those feelings are then referred outward in the actor's body in dialogue, in body movements, in facial expressions, in the actor's thinking (reflected primarily in the actor's face), and in the actor's handling of everyday artifacts, or "props." The audience senses—primarily sees and hears—those outer physical dynamics of the actor's performance and then unconsciously remembers and activates through its own muscle memory the emotions that gave them birth in their own lives.

"Muscle memory" is the term used for the physical repository of experiences imprinted in an individual's and group of individuals' neural patterns. These neural repositories of physical and emotional experiences—physical and emotional memories —are our personal and species record keeping, our neural memories of the outer physical behaviors and the inner emotions that originally gave them birth. They are the enormous and instantaneously accessible hard drive of our human experience.

The audience sees and hears the actor's voice sound angry, hears the actor say "I hate you" in a tense and strong tone, sees the angry tension in the actor's face, hands and shoulders … and a subliminal sensory memory-identification occurs in the audience. The actor's performance causes the audience to feel similarly to how they felt in their past when they, the audience, manifest such physicalization.

In the process of kinesthesia, however, in this sensory symbiosis of audience member to actor, the shared muscle memory of physical events is not limited by the need for tracing-paper replication. The audience's neural circuits do not have to remember specifically falling off a cliff or being punched in the face to identify emotionally with the actor's experience of such events.

For both the actor and audience member alike, imprinted in our muscle memory is the emotional/physical sensation of falling or sustaining a blow, so, when the actor's body muscularity reacts to the falling over a cliff or sustaining a blow to the face, the abstraction of the physical form and energy in the actor's physical activities causes the emotional identification and stirrings to occur in the audience.

In the kinesthetic process, sights and sounds are reduced to their elemental, shape-abstracted components, and the audience's sensing of those universal, elemental forms becomes the true agent of transmittal. That is why and how audiences remember great performances. They remember how profoundly they have experienced themselves through kinesthesia when the great actors have acted. The great actor's work is remembered not only because of what she said and did, but also because she was the transmittal agent through kinesthesia of the audience's own deepest and most profound emotional self-recognition.

B. The Possibility of Reality in Good Acting

How is it possible for actors to have a "real" living performance when, in point of fact, an actor has read the script many times, performed the same story repeatedly, and/or said the same dialogue to the same people endlessly in rehearsal? Are actors miracle workers, gods capable of creating infinite and perpetually renewable lives?

Actors are better than gods: they are Peter Pan-like children who never grow up. Santa Claus is always part of an actor's life on stage. The Easter Bunny is always alive. Big brother is always capable of convincing little brother that the bogeyman is in the closet and that ghosts are in the graveyard or haunted house … and vice versa.

Uncle Sammy can pull the nose off an actor's face time and time again, and the actor believes it, especially when Uncle shows it to her by sticking his thumb out from between his fingers. Actors, like children, believe—time and again—until the curtain falls or the film director yells "Cut." Actors-as-children retain the capacity to exist in a magical, child-imagining, self-perpetual state of reality they are able to turn on and off at will. This capability, creating and maintaining the state of renewable and perpetual childlike innocence, is a central aspect of the actor's talent.

To achieve spontaneity in the face of predictability, to maintain innocence in the face of foreknowledge, to exhibit free will in the face of determinism, is nothing more or less than that which happens to all of us—adults and children alike—in everyday life.

Who among us in our everyday life hasn't had the same (dare I say "childish") fight time and time again with the same partner, even to the extent of hurling the same arguments back and forth at each other: accusations of betrayals, slovenliness, and a lack of consideration? If you are anything like me, you not only have had the experiences, but you also have felt you were having these exchanges "by the numbers," that the event was scripted. Yet, each time—at least in my family life—the arguments retained their emotional freshness, spontaneity, and urgency. Each time, my partner and I perspired; each time, our hearts pumped the same increased level of adrenalin, as we shouted the same recognizable dialogue fast and furiously between us. The argument erupted as if happening for the very first time, as if, each time, we held the same firm belief: "This time, I will be able to get the &%@$ to understand!"

Acting is Living

All human beings strive to live freely in a *predetermined* world.

Death is inevitable, yet we live our daily dramas in a constant state of denial—or at least monumental self-deception—by believing we can change our destiny in the face of certain foreknowledge.

Human beings believe they have unlimited choice and can alter the various unavoidable acts leading up to the end. They believe they can escape the inescapable human script of each and every one of us. They believe they can circumvent their written plot, the ritual stages of life: birth, childhood, puberty, adolescence, adulthood, old age. True, some of the dialogue has yet to be uttered, some of the smaller scenes have yet to be formed, but the major scenes are pre-constructed.

In spite of life's inevitabilities, we act every day as if we have infinitely elastic options, as if we can choose or change our destinies, alter the outcome, opt in or out of life's scripted text. Immortality and perpetual good health are just around the corner; illness and death happen to the other person.

Believing in the power of our individual free will, we mightily try to perpetuate ourselves, and in so doing try to impose our desires for immortality on even the most rigid of life's inevitabilities. We strive to conquer death; we fight the ravages of time and disintegration with the endless possibilities of modern medicine. We believe God will grant us immortality if we operate on this earth with goodness and faith.

"Look on my works, Ye mighty, and despair…" is the stark and dark lesson about life from the poet Shelley's great work, *Ozymandias*. Shelley sensed that we humans are specks of sand on a speck of sand riding through an infinite universe; yet, in spite of his admonition and bleak warning of inevitable decay, we humans live by denying that truth. We must believe that we are essentially important and will sustain ourselves infinitely in the face of an infinitely expanding universe and our finite death.

Just so, an actor confronting a script's inevitability is the same as an everyday human being confronting the inevitability of life itself: free will doing battle with the inexorability of scripted determinism. One of the best definitions of tragedy I know is "fighting against the inexorable."

A good actor in performance is the universe's child, a bursting, ever-growing ball of expanding cellular activity. She has achieved no physical boundaries, so she accepts no operational limitations. Innocence is glory. Life is an infinitely upward and outward adventure in unlimited possibilities. The world is invented anew each time the child-actor awakens, each day the sun comes up fresh and unexpectedly.

In each and every performance, an actor is innocent and young again. Her mind is a clean slate; she is able to act today without foreknowledge of last night's performance. Each new performance is an unique wonder to behold. From performance to performance, life is always novel; life is always original. Change is always achievable; freshness is … on the next page.

This capacity of good actors to achieve the self-hypnotic state of perpetual hope and repeated innocence, night after night, performance after performance, film take after film take, was most strikingly brought home to me several years ago in a class I conducted in San Francisco.

A young lady had just completed enacting a tumultuous love scene in which she tried to keep a lover from abandoning her. At the end of the scene, the lover—as the script so designated—said goodbye. The actress sank to the couch, emitting truly felt, great chest-heaving personal tears of loss. I watched her a long moment, mesmerized by the depth and reality of her grief.

Finally, I said, "Cut." My assistant turned the camera off. The young lady arose from the couch, tears still in her eyes. "I want to do the scene again."

I was shocked. "Why?" I inquired. "Your performance was wonderful. What would you want to do differently?"

She looked me squarely in the eyes, the pain engendered by her performance still apparent, and said, "I'm going to make the bastard stay this time."

Victory—like love—is another performance away.

Some Student Challenges to Reality Acting

"The words are not mine; someone else wrote them."

Assuming that the actor can create reality by believing that every performance of every scene is a fresh experience, what about some other aspects of seeming performance unreality, such as the fact that the dialogue is written by someone else and memorized in advance. Does that reality mitigate against performance reality?

All uttered words were originally conceived by someone else and taught to us. Humans may have a language instinct, but the specific language we speak predates us. None of us born in England, Australia, New Zealand, South Africa, or the United States, were born with English language fluency to express our feelings. It was not part of our genetic inheritance: we all learned English words and phrases from others.

Vocabulary and grammar are learned. All human speech, on stage or off, is memorized. When actors are required to speak a specific language to express their feelings, they are doing nothing more than what all humans being do in everyday life, only more precisely.

In my everyday life, I am often called upon to restrict my array of language and feelings to what I and society deem appropriate. I delimit my vocabulary according to the context; for example, no cancer jokes in a hospice, no cuss words around parents, and no nastiness to my boss.

When I am acting, I am simply called upon to further restrict my language. I must learn not only to say something specific in English about a certain topic, but I must feel like saying just these particular specific scripted English words about this particular topic and release them in this particular grammatical flow, whether I'm in a hospital, on stage, on a set, or at a filmed meeting.

The good actor, confronted with the narrow restrictions of memorized dialogue, says, "No problem. I've been learning dialogue and grammar all my life. Now, as an actor, I will learn to live verbally comfortable and spontaneous, on stage or on screen, within even more narrow language and space restrictions. What do you want me to say—specifically? I have developed the capacity to feel like saying whatever you want."

"The actor playing my husband is not my husband; in fact, I don't really like him, and I cannot pretend that I do."

When I am challenged by a student's statement like that, I often ask a hypothetical question. "Is it possible for you, actor, and that other actor playing your husband—whom you say 'you can't stand'—to have an affair during the filming, and then, six months later, get married? Stop. Think before you answer. I didn't ask if you desired it; I asked if it is hypothetically possible. Yes, hypothetically; right? Thank you for your honesty. Now consider that if you have the capacity to fall in love with him in six months, why can't you achieve the same state in six minutes, or however long the scene takes?"

The answer to the student's problem is fear: fear of being emotionally hurt, fear of making a fool of oneself. Fear is the reason in everyday life why it takes six months, rather than six minutes, to "get to know one another" before engaging in intimacy. Fear breeds caution; overcoming caution takes time.

However, a good actor learns to live fearlessly ... instantly. Time is of the essence, so a good actor banishes personal fear and achieves in six minutes what might take others six months to overcome: to have a one night stand with a stranger, to find loving qualities in a husband when initially (as the actor or actress) only repellent qualities were felt, or manifest repellent qualities in a scene partner when the other actor is an offstage saint.

The key to learning instant intimacy is to banish fear ... quickly.

"How do you expect me to act so privately in public? Isn't it a contradiction in terms?"

Acting privately in public is precisely what everybody does every day of their lives. An actor simply does it in front of larger numbers of people.

Have you ever stood up and cheered at a football game or yelled at your kids in a crowded department store? Or become so involved in a heated conversation on a crowded train that you weren't even aware of the man sitting next to you, much less aware of the ninety other commuters avidly listening and watching you? How many times in a public restaurant have you engaged in a discussion so intimate and private that you didn't hear—until ten minutes after closing time—the vacuum cleaner whirring or see the waiter standing next to the table eager for you to rise and exit?

Acting requires nothing more than something we do in those everyday life situations, only better, fuller, more precisely, and on demand.

I remember one evening being in a restaurant and arguing with my wife, who was telling me not to talk so loud. "Everyone is watching and listening," she admonished.

"I don't care!" I said, continuing to talk too loudly, too involved in the passion of our discussion to care about the audience. (I was, obviously, an actor.)

> *"What do I know about emotions that I've never experienced;*
> *for example, the feeling of being a king or having a child?"*

Acting is not about factual reality; it is about emotional reality.

Have you ever awakened in the middle of the night dripping sweat because of a nightmare? The nightmare wasn't real, nor did the facts in the dream actually occur, but the absence of factual reality didn't preclude the occurrence of real feeling, did it?

The nightmare may have even been phantasmagorical, beyond the bound of rational possibility, but you felt the event deeply nonetheless. Your body literally experienced those feelings, even to the point later, when you related the nightmare to a friend, you probably had the same feelings all over again. Welcome to the world of writing, acting, and imagination, and the possibility of an auto-suggestible, self-induced, emotional reality, irrespective of factual reality.

The History of Reality Acting

The requirement of real-emotional-life-in-acting—onstage performance as a narrow and precise form of everyday emotional life—has always been present in good acting.

In the history of Western Civilization drama, from the Greeks to the Romans to the Renaissance to today, the greatest acting has always been emotionally true to life; always Shakespeare's "mirror up to nature." Great acting has always been onstage, real, emotional life itself, regardless of the epoch, period, styles, restricted parameters, or the staged presentations of that life, including all those epochs when the great actors lacked any psychological understanding of how they attained that real life onstage.

In the earliest stages of acting history, actors were mostly unaware of the precise origins of an actor's real emotions, what could be called today a human's inner self. A living performance was seen as mind-boggling, beyond rational comprehension.

Real, passionate acting, when it occurred, was believed to occur serendipitously, fortuitously; a great performance was sourced outside the actor's control.

In the earliest days of Greek theater, when a great actor created real life onstage and moved audiences to paroxysms of "catharsis"—Aristotle's release of pity and fear—great actors were often considered "inspired by the Muses" (the Ancient Greek gods of the arts), or "touched by the gods," or "divinely inspired." In the Middle Ages, when actors created moving, vivid, life-like performances, their talent was often seen as "touched," "mad," or "possessed by the Devil."

For centuries, it was considered implausible that an actor could create a new, fresh, spontaneous, and believable acting state without supra-human intervention. There must be external causation: emotionally-real acting must be other-worldly, God- or Devil-induced. As a consequence, reality-creating actors were often ostracized by proper society. Actors were seen as one step up from whores, those other great "fakirs" of emotional performance.

Millennia passed while actors searched for logical tap roots into their great acting. They instinctively knew that great acting was inner-conceived, but they didn't understand its precise origins. They were hungry to understand their craft and replicate it in a more knowledgeable, efficacious manner. They wanted to have the ways of the Muses and Gods be known to man, daring to steal acting fire from Zeus.

With little understanding of the psychological and emotional factors underpinning their art, their efforts led more often to concentrating on and/or emulating the outer physical manifestations of other great actor's efforts. They felt that if they duplicated the way great actors' voices sounded, the way their bodies moved, their facial expressions, their own great acting would arise. Walk like a duck, talk like a duck, and become a duck.

Accordingly, a physical vocabulary of great actors' acting manner and mannerisms developed and became increasingly codified. Aspiring actors were taught how to replicate great actors' physical, external vocabulary. This practice of duplicating outer form became a standard teaching methodology, "The Medium is the Message," centuries before our time.

Acting is Living

Teaching-by-replication methodology was not confined to young actors, however, as young Renaissance apprentice painters were required literally to copy the line and texture of a master artist for many years before being allowed to venture out on their own. The theory was to walk in the general shoes of greatness and your individual greatness would more readily follow.

It must be conceded that some actors did achieve great acting by the application of the "physical vocabulary" method. They created real emotional life in their acting by mimicking the form of great actors, but their achievement was unaware and inconsistent. They were subject to the God of Luck.

For the great mass of uninspired or unlucky actors who were trained in the regimented "physical vocabulary" methodologies —without being unconsciously inspired to inwardly feel at the same time—much coldly-sculpted "presentational acting" resulted. Great form was replicated, but the actor's inner feelings remained absent. Body, voice, face, and gesture were consciously manipulated by the actor—sometimes brilliantly—but the resultant performances were often wooden, stilted, and dead of human feeling … which thereby lessened the possibility of deep emotional kinesthesia with the audience.

(Working in this manner today, from the outside in, remains a valid path of acting preparation and education. It is often called the "British system," as opposed to the "American-Russian system." In the British system, form is used to create substance; in the America-Russian system, the actor's inner emotion is activated first and outer expressiveness follows.)

In the late nineteenth century, due to the seminal discoveries of the human psyche's inner workings by psychiatrists such as Freud, Jung, Adler et al—and their theoretical detailing of emotion's ties to the unconscious and the human primitive limbic system—a systematic, methodological approach to creating emotionally real acting became feasible. By exploiting new psychological knowledge, actors were increasingly able to define, understand and create psychologically-based acting techniques and exercises that better prepared them to more predictably and efficiently create real emotional life on stage—thereby wedding great inner emotional substance to great outer form on a dependable, programmatic basis.

Contemporary Reality Acting

In the latter half of the nineteenth century, the brilliant Russian teacher, theorist, and director Stanislavski, the father of the so-called "Method" of acting training, was at his Moscow Art Center directing, rehearsing, and performing plays by Anton Chekhov, the great late-nineteenth century Russian playwright (*Three Sisters, The Sea Gull, The Boor*). In rehearsal, Stanislavski found the Checkhov plays weren't working because the actor's performances lacked emotional excitement.

Stanislavski respected his actors' talents and instinctively knew that Chekhov was a genius, so he blamed himself for the dullness of the actors' efforts. He felt he was not directing the actors properly enough, not guiding them to mount a production worthy of the actors' talent and Chekhov's writing.

Stanislavski soon determined the problem was the old style of acting and decided that he needed to develop a new style of acting, a style that would enable the otherwise talented actors to take full advantage of what he believed to be the subliminal, subterranean, and deep brilliant emotional life possibilities of a Chekhov character. Stanislavski felt that the truth of a Chekhov performance was found more often not in what the character wasn't saying, rather than in what the character was saying.

The characters in the new realistic plays of Ibsen and Chekhov did not declaim or reveal their inner sentiments in florid language, but refracted their emotions, subdued them, hid them internally, below seeming everyday conversation. Chekhov's and Ibsen's characters onstage spent long periods sitting and talking of commonplace things, such as crops, landscape, and the weather. Stanislavski's acting conundrum: where's the drama—the theatrical excitement—in Chekhov's prosaic surface conversation about crops, landscape, and the weather?

Stanislavski's search for new acting techniques—aimed at stirring and revealing the hidden truth and excitement of a Checkhov character—coincided with the inner psyche discoveries of his contemporary theorist, Sigmund Freud, the father of modern psychoanalysis, who was doing seminal work on the inner touchstones of human passion, uncovering in his psychoanalytic sessions with patients the ties between sensory experience, memories, and inner emotion.

Using the psychological discoveries of Freud (and others), Stanislavski devised a series of acting exercises and techniques to stimulate inner feelings in actors. Everything the actor did in the subsequent performance, however small, however commonplace —all the ordinary doings and sayings of a Chekhov character— literally vibrated with inner passion and meaning.

Hold out your right hand, palm down; now place your left hand directly below it and push up. Be energetic. Push hard, but keep the right hand stationary. Notice the resultant tension in the right hand's effort. That is the surface tension in a Checkhov play and where the Stanislavski cum Freud emotionally-inducing new acting methods lay: in the strong emotions activated beneath—yet threatening to explode upward—through the seemingly calm, ordinary, flat Chekhovian dialogue.

Stanislavski's series of emotional exercises and techniques set in motion the feeling whirlpool beneath the actor's calm surface; methods calculated to make sure the calm hand of the actor is vibrating with inner emotional ecstasy while, at the same time, the hand is being held level.

He tirelessly trained his Moscow actors to activate in themselves (prior to performance) the deepest of the actors' personal, unresolved passions, awakening and uncovering the emotional experiences often deposited deeply in the actor's psyches. When these actors-as-characters performed the commonplace occurrences of a Checkhov piece, in the smallest gesture of a Chekhov stage direction, in the most innocent comment of Chekhovian dialogue, the actor-as-character's calm surface behavioral performance vibrated with the actor's deepest and most unresolved inner turmoil (always appropriate to the dictates of script, of course).

Small Talk

Years ago, my wife and I often went to our favorite pie shop in Santa Monica, California, one frequented by many senior citizens. We invariably ate our pie, happily chattering away, while we saw around us many older couples eating their pie in complete silence.

One evening, in the full flush of youth, I said in my most superior manner, "I hope that when we get old, we still have something left to say." She assured me we would.

Time passes.

My wife and I are now of pie-eating age, and most of the time we eat in silence also, which led me to wonder if we finally have reached the age where we also have nothing to say? No, I determine, the opposite is true: we have too much to say. (The following scene is all fictional, of course.)

"Pretty day, isn't it?" I say, as we sit at a window booth in the pie shop.

"Oh, sure," she says, "but not so pretty that I could get you away from the TV and those damn football games. It was an even nicer day yesterday and I wanted to go to the ocean, but no, you couldn't pry yourself away from the football game to accompany me…."

I become silent and decide to cease talking about the weather and eat my pie. I see the waitress. "I'd like some ice cream on my pie," I say to her.

"Ice cream?!" my wife says. "We can't even afford your cholesterol medicine! If you had taken better care of yourself when you were young, instead of eating eggs twice a day every day…. I told you…!"

I decide there will be no ice cream, no waitress, no more small talk. I will maintain a long period of silence.

"Isn't that a cute couple?" she finally says, looking at a boy and a girl who look much as we did many years ago.

"Cute?" I explode derisively. "He's got buck teeth. He looks like that guy you had the affair with! Speaking of which, I saw the S.O.B. last week. It's twenty-two years later, and I still don't know what you saw in him. If you hadn't been so out of control …!"

Small talk (Chekhovian or otherwise) is the time-honored way to avoid big talk. Saying little, next-to-nothing—silence—skirts the unresolved passion that too often vibrates beneath the surface of our smallest comment, incident, or most commonplace gesture of our everyday life. The passionate past always hovers under the seeming safety of innocuous small talk and threatens to erupt in the most unexpected and seemingly inconsequential manner, which is exactly what Freud discovered—lurking within our deep psyches—over a century ago, and Stanislavski trained his actors to activate.

We engage in small talk to avoid shearing the top off our smoldering, volcanic, inner life with a misplaced word, gesture, or action. When you go to dinner with a couple who have had a fight the moment before your arrival, their smallest gesture vibrates with their inner tension and anger. It is a most uncomfortable dinner to be participating in ... or the most wonderful performance to witness in the theater!

Stanislavski's acting discoveries—exercises and techniques to programmatically arouse and heighten an actor's inner passion—led to brilliant performances of Chekhov's and subsequent modern realistic plays, including those of O'Neill, Miller, Williams, and Pinter, among any others. Emotional reality in modern acting found its contemporary seed and flowered in the fertile soil of the dual discoveries of these two giants: Freud and Stanislavski.

Stanislavski's fame spread rapidly, most notably to America, where a band of actors, teachers, and directors centered in New York, at numerous institutions such as the Group Theater, The Actor's Studio, Neighborhood Playhouse, HB Studio—as well as innumerable other like-minded training centers—further developed the Stanislavski method of working. His and his followers' exercises and techniques soon became known—for better and for worse—as "The Method."

C. Reality and the Nerve Cell

All right, you've convinced me that good acting is real, living, emotional acting, good emotional acting always has been real acting, and good real emotional acting can consistently be achieved in modern times by emotional training and technique.

But if all good acting is simply life, why study this acting text; why do we have to teach *life*? Why teach and study something we already know?

My answer: everyone knows about life, but when people choose to become actors and go on stage or in front of the cameras— when they are placed under the pressure of audience-witnessing —99% of would-be actors forget how to live.

Under the acting demand of living excitingly in front of people with great emotional fervor and within very narrow confines of speech and movement, they forget how to live *in reality*. They stop doing all the things they naturally and automatically do in their everyday life. They stop listening to one another. They stop talking to one another. They stop converting stimuli into feelings, and they stop allowing feelings to inform their outer actions. Having lost their sense of reality under the exigencies of public performance pressure, they need to create false reality— bad acting—to fill the onstage void.

For the beginning actor—and for the acting teacher of beginning actors—the chore becomes how to tutor the unreal or beginning actor to repeat in performance the student's sense of everyday truth, to capture and recapitulate how to operate in reality, something they implicitly know from their everyday life.

Leonardo da Vinci, the great Renaissance artist and sculptor, found himself similarly knowledge-challenged when he desired to sculpt and paint the human form more truthfully. He realized he was having problems with his paintings because he viewed the human form from outside, subjectively, as it were, but not objectively, clinically, from beneath the skin, which would have provided him with a more specific knowledge of the human form. To obtain a truer vantage point to further his artistic development, he noted, he studied, and he drew—with exactitude—the inner workings of the human form.

Like da Vinci, new actors must consider their inner human reality dispassionately, minutely, and impartially, and thereby become objectively aware how human behavior operates in everyday life so that, when studying acting, they can apply that new knowledge to prepare better to live on stage, *in reality*.

What is Reality?

I haven't the slightest idea what reality is, at least not in any philosophical or essential sense, but I can offer the beginning actor a static description of human reality to logically facilitate the process of turning the beginner's unreal acting into the good actor's *real* acting. That model is ... the human nerve cell.

Human reality starts with, literally and figuratively, a single cell (the Mom and Dad get-together at the my-seed-meets-your-egg level. What can be more basic than that?). The human cell—at its most basic operational core—is a **stimulus→synapse→response** system. A cell is stimulated by events outside itself and sends those sensory signals along neurons that leap across a synaptic gap and create a motor response.

All human behavior, therefore, onstage or off, becomes—for acting analysis purposes—an entity that is capable of being stimulated (seeing, hearing, touching, tasting, and smelling), converts those sensory readings into synapses (or feelings), which then energize themselves outward into responses. In traditional acting theory we call those elements of acting life (1) looking and listening, as well as tasting, smelling and touching, (2) emotions, and (3) actions.

The Primacy of Purpose in Creating Reality

Before we can use this tri-part static definition of a nerve cell as a fundamental fact and learning tool of human operating reality, we must convert its static definition into a dynamic one. We must ask: What existential factor gives that static cellular system its dynamism? Why does a single cell have a stimulus→synapse→response system—the ability to sense, feel, and act on those feelings—in the first place?

When I attended my first acting class in Los Angeles many years ago, I was taught that "Acting is listening," so I tried to open my ears to hear the other actor(s) on stage. I tried to listen to them, to absorb their dialogue, but I inevitably found my novice actor's brain moving to other things. I thought about my performance. I thought about the audience. I became aware of the other students in the room watching me. I too-often thought about my girlfriend at home (we were having problems).

No more than fifteen or twenty seconds from the beginning of the scene, I became so caught up with everything outside the scene on stage that I became unaware of anything in the scene, including the other actor. I even forgot the other actor was onstage with me, much less listened to him. I became a failure at listening.

In the very next class, after a week of self-chastening, I vowed to listen even more intently to my fellow actor(s). "Listen, listen, and listen," I reminded myself. However, once I was onstage, the same pattern evidenced itself. I listened intensely for a while, and then … tuned out.

I further chastised myself: Didn't I want to be an actor?

I wrestled with that inattentiveness syndrome week after week until one day I realized that I don't listen to anyone unless *I want something from them.*

Purpose (or as we refer to it in Chapter 1, *objective*) activates and underscores the total dynamic operation of human cellular function of sensing, feeling, and doing. Purpose becomes the central activating impetus in giving dynamism to the human stimulus→synapse→response mechanism. We sense, we feel, we act ... *to achieve purpose.*

1. Stimulus: The Actor's Need to Look and Listen

To enable the good actor to act with purpose in a real manner—to operate as a real, living human being in pursuit of a dynamic objective—the beginning actor must be taught to pursue objectives through a specific reality. As in everyday life, she must learn to see and hear in detail. The two most important words in an actor's training are "specific" and "active" as they learn to move appropriately—in reality—through their human and physical world.

The Specificity of Stimuli

In Chapter 1, in the discussion of conflict and objectives, we dealt with a character's need to move actively through the world in the pursuit of goals. Now we must also encourage the good actor to move *specifically* through the world of stimuli.

Reality is not general. Evolution—or an intelligently-designed universe—created with great specificity the sensory-feeling-action system of a cell. Real emotion does not occur in a spontaneous, life-like manner (good acting) unless the actor is truly in contact with specific stimuli—sight, sound, smell, taste, and touch—of the world around them.

A story to illustrate: A new actor was given his first role on Broadway: he was a replacement for the role of "A Soldier" in a major Shakespearean production. He had one line: "Hark; I hear the canon!"

That's it; one line: "Hark; I hear the cannon!" It seemed simple enough, so the Stage Manager determined that the actor didn't need to rehearse the line with the director during the week. The actor could just show up on the first night of the engagement and perform.

The actor was excited. All week he rehearsed the line on his own, trying to give the one line different inflections, pauses, and accents, trying to find the best way to deliver the line: "*Hark* ... I *hear* the cannon!" "Hark; I hear *the* cannon!" "Hark! I hear the *cannon*!" "*Hark; I hear the cannon!*"

The moment arrived. The actor appeared at his proper entrance place in the wings, the stage manager looked at him and nodded, and he made his entrance. No sooner had he stepped on stage than a huge BOOM filled the auditorium.

The actor stopped dead in his tracks: "*What the fuck was that?!?*"

As I say ... specific reality creates specific response.

(FINAL NOTE ON STIMULI: In defining the-sensory-world-through-which-the-character-must-move to achieve her goals, traditional acting theory, most acting texts use the term "obstacles," but I prefer to substitute the word "external reality."

The word "obstacles" implies an actor-as-character is always moving through a problematic world, a world filled with unavoidable impediments. The word "obstacles" limits the world to only problems and not possible successes. "External reality," on the other hand, is a neutral term, one that allows for an occasionally benign world, a world subject to triumph, a world that sometimes—when we are in successful contact with it—makes us happy, relieved, and joyous.

External reality is not an "obstacle" until our emotions define it as such.)

The Problem of Repetition

I agree that human behavior (good acting) requires the character to have a purpose, and also requires the actor to really listen and look at the other actors and events in the scene as they pursue that purpose. How can an actor listen and look with fresh ears and fresh eyes, from performance to performance, film take to film take, when (in reality) they have heard all that dialogue before and watched that same person deliver the responding dialogue before? How can the actor maintain visual and auditory specificity after endless repetition?

Good actors maintain a freshness of reality in every performance or film take because they never see the other characters as general faces or listen to the dialogue as general words. On the contrary, they always see *specific* (and ever-changing) facial features, and hear *specific* sounds of words from performance to performance.

In my everyday life, I don't automatically believe everything I hear. I often take words in everyday life with a subjective grain of salt because, in my experience, half the time spoken words—mine and others—tend to obfuscate rather than clarify. They are deniers of the truth more than revealers; so in everyday life I don't simply listen to just the words of someone's conversation. I focus on how the words sound and how the speaker's face looks when speaking.

There is one particular three-word piece of everyday dialogue I have heard a thousand times, "I love you," yet when someone says to me "I love you," each time I hear it freshly. I note—albeit unconsciously—the vocal and physical package surrounding the words. My constant need for real, honest love (the purpose behind my listening) makes me question the intent of the message.

"Did she say 'I love you' sweetly only because I am buying her a new car?"

"Why is she saying 'I love you,' but can't look at me while she is saying it?"

"She said 'I love you' after she drank three glasses of wine. Her eyes are so glazed ... is it love, boredom—or booze—generating the words?"

"Oh, sure, it's easy to say 'I love you' in bed!"

In each performance, when a good actor sees another actor walk through a door to an ever-changing reality, she experiences an ever-changing reality. There invariably are subtle, slight shifts of the actor's body, angles at which the actor-as-character holds her head, a change in whether she looks at the other actor directly or from the side of her eyes. The good actor sees the slight changes in the other actor's face and listens to the ever-changing pitch, tone, rhythm, and volume of the voice. These changes can and will create varying and fresh emotional changes in me due to changing perceptions of the minute differences in you.

2. Synapse: Converting Stimuli into Emotion

"All right," you say, "I get it. I accept good acting as the purpose-driven nerve cell in operation, and, therefore, a good actor must enter a scene with a purpose (an objective). She must try to attain that objective by moving actively and specifically through the external reality from whence she is stimulated.

"Okay, what happens next: purpose, stimulus, and then …?"

Emotions happen next, the second and most important part of the cellular tri-part process. As we purposefully pursue our objectives, we have contact with the specific facts of our external reality, *and we feel*.

Emotions are central to the actor's existence. They create the personal interpretation of the sensory data around us. They make subjective our otherwise neutral, objective life. They give personal (emotional) meaning to our world's external reality. They educate us, inform us, and tell us—through our feelings—whether we are getting what we want or not.

Emotions are the core of acting.

The English word *emotion* is derived from the Middle French word *emouvoir*, meaning to stir up. The seat of emotions is said to be located in the amygdala, or the most primitive limbic system of the brain. As a result, emotion can be viewed as stirring up of the core primitive level of one's basic behavior, activating the foundational neural layer upon which the other human behavioral layers are built. Stirred-up emotion becomes the character's personality down to her primitive atavistic self. Emotions drive a character's inner life, how a person responds characteristically— fundamentally—under pressure.

When we seek to "really know who someone is," what we really are attempting to define is how someone feels, emotionally responds, when we put them under the pressure of specific reality.

Unfortunately, some acting authors speak of only eight basic emotions, as if a human's feelings are limited to an eight-feeling spectrum, a child's box of basic beginner crayons. Good actors, on the other hand, those who want to grow in performance abilities, those who want to color more richly complex and textured character portraits, must increasingly start to understand emotions are overwhelmingly complex, beyond a package of even sixteen colors, beyond even thirty-two, or even the older child's box of sixty-four colors.

The good actor knows, when analyzing a character for performance, that her deepest emotions can never totally be known and predicted in advance of their actualization in rehearsal or performance. Eventually, when fully developed in her craft, a good actor accepts that creating vivid emotional characterizations requires in her performance approach an almost infinite gradation, an unlimited array of emotions.

Emotional Auto-Stimulation

Allow me to make an important distinction between (a) the deeply complex emotions properly created during the scene by the actor's really listening and looking at the other actors-as-characters in the scene, and (b) a bad actor's falsely-arrived-at emotional activation caused by the actor's private, auto-stimulated, auto-induced efforts.

The good actor in performance must always allow the specific realities of the scene to be the activating force behind the emotional experience on set or on stage.

I suggest that any actor keep in mind that real emotion is not an originating event in life; it is secondary (actually, tertiary: purpose→stimuli→*emotions*); therefore, an actor who "plays" an emotion in a scene by itself, as an originating act, with no outer stimuli to activate that emotion—an actor who seeks to auto-stimulate his/her own emotions during the scene, perhaps by erroneously self-applying exercises and techniques mid-scene, thereby activating emotions on their own—is a false actor.

A good actor always remembers to allow outer stimuli of the scene to activate her emotions. Auto-stimulation of emotion in performance may feel like the real thing, but the bad actor should note that nothing in life has ever been created that way.

Emotional Preparation versus Emotional Performance
There is another important emotion-creating distinction to draw between good-acting emotions that properly arise in performance and improperly self-induced emotions that arise in a bad acting performance. There is a contrast between a good actor's process of proper emotional self-activation before a scene, and the emotion that arises during a scene. Emotional preparation, as the phrase implies (the prefix *pre-* means *before*), is preparing emotions before the scene that the actor anticipates might be needed for the character during a scene.

Auto-stimulated emotions that may properly be activated in preparation as long as it is put away prior to performance, held in the body's reservoir, to arise later in performance when stimulated by the external realities in the playing of the scene.

An illustration: a good poker player needs lots of money to enter a high-stakes poker game. In preparation, the player goes to the bank, empties her savings account, fills her pockets with lots of money before the game—$1000 bills, rather than pennies, if she expects the game to be high-stakes and exciting. Exciting poker, like exciting acting, is an expensive game to play.

Once the poker game begins, however, she operates logically, that is, she does not play the game eager to spend her money. In fact, her goal is quite the opposite: to spend as little of her own money as the tactics of the game (*conflict*) require for her to win.

Emotional Preparation Exercises

How the actor prepares emotionally for performance before the scene may be enhanced by time-honored emotional preparation techniques and exercises actors can use so rich, emotional stimulation can best occur during—and due to the events of—the scene. These actor preparation exercises and techniques compare to a safe-cracker rubbing her emotional fingertips raw with sandpaper to better sensitize her for the external realities that she will confront in pursuit of the objective: to better feel the lock's click in the upcoming safe-cracking effort.

Personalization

In everyday life, we may say to someone who takes emotional affront to some words or action "Don't take it personally," hoping that, by depersonalizing an experience, extreme emotional activation will be avoided. Good actors, on the other hand, who always seek to heighten their potential pool of emotional susceptibility, make sure the exact opposite applies. Good actors-as-characters prepare to take everything personally, as if all the events of the scene are important and really happening to them. This acceptance of personal importance creates the actor's heightened potential for personal emotional involvement in the scene. (SEE more on "Importance" in Chapter 6: "Intensity.")

Substitution

Uta Hagen, the great actress and teacher, strongly proposed in her very insightful book, *Respect for Acting*, another emotional preparation technique: "Substitution." Webster's Dictionary defines substitution as "the act of putting a person or thing in place of another serving the same purpose; to take the place of…." (An enlightened student of mine once defined all acting as "putting one's self into someone else's shoes.")

Ms. Hagen offers her own definition of "substitution" as "… taking a substituted psychological reality and transferring it to the existing circumstances and events in the play; transferring the [emotional] essence of the experience to the scene."

In applying Ms. Hagen's technique, the actor asks, "What do the character, the story, and I—in my everyday experience—have in common, perhaps not relative to the events of the scene, but in an analogous, metaphorically emotional way?

"In my personal life," the actor muses in applying this technique, "are there any persons, places things—and their attendant emotions—that I have experienced similar to persons, places, things, and emotions the character in the scene has to go through?"

If the answer is yes, the actor can *substitute* the personal experience for the scripted experience in order to better activate the required potential pool of emotions which will later be required for the scene.

For example: "The scene calls for me to hate my husband in the scene, but I find it hard to hate any husband because I love my husband. I love all husbands, in fact.

"However, every time I think of my abusive Uncle Harry, I feel inordinate hate … so I'll substitute my feelings for my Uncle Harry for the desired feelings for my husband in the scene."

Or: "Later in the scene, when I'm expected to be scared of tunnels; I think 'I like tunnels. They don't scare me, but…a spider scares the hell out of me, so I'll substitute a room filled with big spiders to prepare for the frightened emotion necessary for the tunnel scene.'"

Emotional Recall

"Emotional recall" is another preparation exercise similar to substitution, except that the actual physical experience of a particular emotion is recalled, opposed to simply recalling specific people, places and things that caused the past emotional experience. In emotional recall, the actor specifically remembers how it felt when re-experiencing the emotion.

Emotional recall, sometimes called "affective memory" or "emotional memory," is actors remembering—in physical, specific detail—the actual physical sensations of a particular emotion, and that memory activates the specific emotion in the actor.

Given Circumstances

"Given Circumstances" is a technique for activating an actor's potential for emotion by having the actor simply accept the given circumstances of the script, to "buy in" to the writer's specific plot points and events. This technique of emotional preparation focuses on the actor's imagination as an emotional technique to activate the appropriate emotion in the actor. Stanislavski called it the technique of "The Magic If…?" "What if something like the events of the scene happens to me in everyday life? How would I feel?"

Cliff Osmond

Prior History

Prior history is another emotional preparation exercise wherein the actor:

1. Focuses initially on the past history of the character as stip-
    ulated in the script; for example, how long has that charac-
    ter been married, were they raised rich or poor, are they
    college graduates? The actor then asks: what are the emo-
    tions that probably have been activated and highlighted in
    the character's past because of those experiences? The ac-
    tor, thus prepared by a review of the character's past expe-
    riences, can then enter the scene as an emotionally
    stimulated mix of all that has gone before.

2. In order to encourage further emotional openness in an
    actor-as-character prior to the entrance into a scene, actors
    sometimes are asked to fill in imaginatively the factual gaps
    of a character's past life that may have been left out of the
    script, thus stimulating—through the actor's story imagina-
    tion—a stream of felt emotions.

3. A combination of the above two becomes:

    *"My character got married (in the script) because she (this is not in
    the script) was pregnant, but a week after the marriage (fact in the
    script), her husband talked her into an abortion (not in the script);"*

    or ...

    *"My character is wealthy (in the script), having inherited vast sums
    from her father's estate ...but (this is not in the script) she secretly
    hates him because her father was never home. He was arrested for
    stock fraud and spent six months in jail, and she has always felt
    betrayed."*

Imagined prior history works very well as an emotional exercise because it forces the actor to stir up their own emotions to create imaginative character histories. After all, who is doing the factual imagining: the actor?! It is not surprising that imagined histories often reflect the actor's personal emotional history.

The Moment Before

Another emotional preparation technique, "The Moment Before," could be called "The Most Immediate Prior History," a technique that recognizes that the character's present emotional state is more affected by recent history (what happened just prior to the scene) than distant history (what happened in earlier scenes).

If, for example, just before entering the scene, the character has been rushing through aggravating mid-town traffic, or climbing a long flight of stairs, or regurgitating in the hallway just prior to a knock at the door, upon entrance into the scene, the emotions arising from these *most* proximate series of events dominate the actor-as-character's *less* proximate experiences. It is similar to the "LIFO" inventory accounting method: "Last In, First Out." Recent emotional history trumps past emotional history: the good actor prepares to enter the scene in the emotional state most highly activated by the most preceding events.

As Ye Emotionally Sow, So Shall Ye Emotionally Reap

When an actor, preparatory to entering a scene as a character, uses any emotional exercise or technique to highly-activate one particular script-dictated emotion, or script-dictated set of emotions over others, she can really be viewed as disrupting her own personal balance (assuming she has one in her everyday life!) to create an emotional excess or imbalance consistent with the life of the character.

For example: in the scripted or imagined past, the actor analyzing a character's emotional needs may contemplate the mother
who beat the character in the script, the father who ignored her,
the sister who was prettier, the husband who divorced her, or the
sweet loving family who nurtured her but is now dead. This con-
templation of scripted events creates an overwhelming weight
on one side of the actor-as-character's emotional teeter-totter,
heightening a particular set of emotional baggage that the actor-
as-character will carry into the scene, causing that side of her
emotional personality to become dominant, unbalanced relative
to the other.

The unbalanced actor-as-character enters the scene in a state of
emotional disequilibrium (emotionally unbalanced characters are
always exciting for the audience to watch) and the audience
watches as they seek to reassert balance through their character's
objective path.

Seen in this light, the character's objective in any scene becomes
the method by which the actor-as-character seeks to re-establish
emotional homeostasis or contentment.

Mini Summary: Stimuli and Emotions

Let us, for a brief moment, review the acting paradigm laid out so far. The actor—in preparation for being the actor-as-character—uses one or more emotional preparation techniques to activate the emotions necessary to create that character-demanded imbalance.

Once properly destabilized, the actor-as-character enters the scene and seeks a specific objective, which is her purposeful, active attempt to redress the past, to find a renewed balance in her emotional life. That objective quest is always in diametric opposition to the objective(s) of the other character(s) in the scene.

In pursuing their objectives, all on-stage or on-set, actors-as-characters confront each other—and their overall external reality—with their five senses (primarily listening and looking). Confronting that external reality thusly, the stimuli from the scene activates all the actors-as-characters' emotions that are drawn from the emotional potentials created in their respective (and prepared) pasts. These feelings, inner chemical and electronic flows, once activated, then move on their eventual path outward toward overt expressions, creating an actors' subsequent actions.)

3. Motor Response: Converting Emotion into Action

Motor response (actions), the third element in the tri-part definition of a cell, are the human systemic attempt to harness and channel inner synaptic emotion (activated by stimuli) into direct (or indirect) outer activity, always, of course, recognizing that these actions are created to forward our overall purpose.

Emotions are the explosive gunpowder set afire by the triggering mechanism of stimuli, but they cry out for the encasement of the shell (the action) to give those feelings power, purposeful aim, and trajectory. "I feel like saying…," or "I feel like taking a walk," or "I feel like throwing a glass of water in his face" are not just figurative statements: they are literal truth. Stimuli-activated inner feelings morph into outer actions to serve our purposes.

The Five Categories of Action

These five categories of actions are the external mechanisms by which human beings create and channel (and thereby reveal kinesthetically to an audience) feelings. They become the external performance reality by which the audience has its own emotions stimulated.

Actions—doing—the organizing of emotion into outer purposeful tactics, the way emotion is released and revealed to the outer world, has five (5) basic categories:

1. *Dialogue* has two constituent parts: (1a) words, ideas that are arranged into symbols and syntax, and (1b) voice, how we physically/vocally manifest those words;

2. *Large body movements* include all major bodily physical movements carried out by legs and trunk;

3. *Facial reactions and other small bodily gestures*, primarily eyes, mouth, head, shoulders, hands and arms, the localized small body movements that can often be considered non-verbal statements, attitudes, and non-verbal expressions;

4. *The handling of props*, the manner in which we handle the everyday artifacts of human life. (The word *props* is a theater word for *property*. "Property of 'XYZ' Theater" was originally stamped on such theatrical artifacts as snuff boxes, fans, glasses, dishes, bottles, and other items that belonged to the theatrical company that owned them.);

5. *Thought*, the final component of human actions/expressiveness (4½, if you prefer), is a step interposed between emotion and outer released action. Human thoughts are inner ideas stimulated by emotions that never quite make it out of the mouth into words. We feel, we think, but (consciously or unconsciously) tactically we choose not to say.

Action #1: Dialogue
Words

The verbal part of an actor's action performance (words as actions) is the least important of the actor's motor response concerns.

If words were the critical and most important component in an actor's performance, the actor would be asked to make up his own (reality shows notwithstanding). Instead, dialogue is almost always written by someone else and given to to actor, just as the play's or film's costumer gives the actor clothes, the make-up person gives her make-up, or the prop co-coordinator gives her props to use.

As a result, words/dialogue should be considered as a *pre-conceived* and *pre-designed* action—created by someone else—to arm the actor with the instrumentality (ideas) for the ensuing conflict. The actor's task essentially becomes to activate the words with personal emotion and to bring the memorized words to the performance to use as tactics in the ongoing struggle.

If actors during an audition rely merely on saying the words on the printed page to be their performance focus, they are going to fail. The words of the script are not being auditioned. The truth is that every actor in an audition says the same words. The auditioner, therefore, to stand out and succeed must emphasize the other aspects in an actor's performance: feelings, voice, face, body, all the things that are not given to the actor, but that distinguish, in performance, one actor from another actor.

Voice

Voice is the second aspect of an actor's dialogue performance, the sound-delivery system of the words. Words are formed outwardly by air expulsion resulting from diaphragm activity and lung activity in concert with voice box maneuvering, tongue placement, and mouth shaping.

Similar to the rest of the actor's body, the sound of the voice is activated by emotion. However, only in rare and selective instances in the script does the author suggest how the voice is to operate and the emotion from which the words/ideas are to flow.

Accordingly, the author might add above a line of dialogue, "She says sadly," "She says huskily," "She says angrily," "She says loudly," but, in most instances, the emotion (and tone) behind the utterance is almost exclusively left up to the actor to determine—and her emotional system operating in performance.

Vocal Scoring: A Dangerous Rehearsal Technique

Some actors are taught (improperly) in rehearsal or preparation to "score the text," to mark in pen or pencil each individual line of the text with chosen notations of accent, rising inflection, elongated vowels, and so on, to anticipate and prepare specifically how they are going to say the lines in performance.

Warning: Dialogue scoring is a dangerous form of acting preparation because it more often than not leads to stilted, false, and predetermined replication of vocal rehearsal choices in subsequent performance. Such rigid predetermination all too often creates in the actor a subsequent presentational performance that is devoid of emotion and merely a replication of a previously imagined and scored reality (in rehearsal), and that leaves no room for unexpected, real, spontaneous emotions to occur in a proper performance.

While it is true that dialogue, in preparation, should be analyzed as to intellectual content, logic and meaning, and evaluated as to emotional sourcing, scripts should never be precisely "scored" as to the eventual performance desires. It is logical and proper to anticipate certain feelings and actions to occur, but the actor must leave room for the surprisingly fuller, richer, and spontaneous reality, the final tone, pitch, and rhythm of the ensuing dialogue, that can and must occur in performance.

The Writer's Scoring

Writers sometimes suggest in the script the emotion they'd like the actor to feel when delivering a line of dialogue. "She says huskily," they write above the dialogue, thereby trying to dictate to the actor how they want the line said and felt. Sometimes the writer underlines a particular word or uses CAPS (all capital letters) to suggest to the actor that the writer wants the word emphasized in the actor's vocal delivery. The same holds with exclamation point(s) at the end of a sentence!!! Sometimes writers include ellipsis in the writing of the dialogue: "I love you ... very much ...," to indicate the dialogue is cast with tentativeness, an air of uncertainty, or lack of definitiveness. The use of double-dashes at the end of a piece of dialogue often suggests that the actor-as-character is interrupted by another character's dialogue.

These suggestions reflect the writer's desire to direct the actor's vocal performance. Actors should see such scripted indications not as definitive commands, but as welcomed suggestions from a fellow creative artist to be considered, respected, and initially rehearsed, but ultimately dismissed if the actor finds her line-delivery choices (and their underlying emotional motivations) more honest—or more appealing—in actual performance.

Directorial Scoring

Likewise, directors in rehearsal often give actors very specific, detailed line readings to tell actors how they want the line to be said: what accent, what intonation, what volume. In these cases, the director says the line first to indicate to the actor how she wants it said in performance, "dialogue-scoring" the actor's performance.

Two possible explanations of that explicit director's line reading effort can be considered. The first explanation is that the director may be indirectly communicating to the actor a general feeling for the dialogue, using her offering of the dialogue line reading as a substance-indicating shorthand. The director hopes that her reading of the line activates the actor's feelings similar to the emotional substance the director desires the actor-as-character to feel.

The other interpretation is that the director considers actors as puppets-on-the-string. The martinet director offers precise, predetermined performance readings not as emotional shorthand suggestions, but to indicate the precise tone, accent, and rhythm the actor is expected to duplicate in performance.

Directors such as that should be treated respectfully and in the following manner: in subsequent rehearsal or performance, the actor should deliver the line according to the actor's sense of emotional reality and nothing else. If the director is left unsatisfied and feels forced to reiterate the demand in another performance, the actor should reply: "Didn't I say it the way you wanted?! Let me try again."

Martinets, directors or otherwise, sooner or later wear out.

The Reality-Trap in Dialogue Memorization

Actors are often just as guilty of being their own directorial martinets and imposing line readings on themselves during rehearsal memorization. The reason for such dangerous behavior is pragmatic: repeated rhythm, cadence and intonation aid the actor in dialogue memory.

Song lyrics are generally easier to memorize than dialogue because the constant rhythm of the music, the steadiness of form and the repetitive emotion underlying the lyrics, help the mind to retain the words. Similarly, an actor who seeks the same ease of memorization often practices line readings with a chosen accent, rhythm, and intonation, and set, accordingly, their line readings. However, there is a price to pay for this mnemonic aid because these memorized and over-practiced line-readings from rehearsal, when faithfully repeated in performance, almost always lead to stilted, dead presentational (bad) acting.

Learning lines is a difficult task, and the use of mnemonic crutches may be understandable at first, but good actors must eventually memorize the lines beyond the mnemonic crutch of initial line readings. Ideally, they must become capable in later rehearsal and performance of speed work, saying the words flatly and fast, without intonation, rhythm, or accent. Only when an actor knows the dialogue in this fashion can an actor truly be said to know her lines. Only then do the lines become flexible action elements for subsequent use in the actor's performance.

I remember—a painful memory—acting in a particular TV Western. I had decided in rehearsal at home to memorize my lines in a manner suited to what I thought would be as scripted: a quiet scene in a barn. I planned a series of line readings that were slow, tentative, quiet, and meaningful, but when I got to the set, the director decided that the scene would not be set in a barn but would be acted and filmed on horse, riding fast, during a shootout. Accordingly, he wanted the dialogue to be delivered fast. Believe me; my rehearsal memorization was really put to the test. Not only did I have trouble riding a horse, but I forgot most of my dialogue until "take" twelve. The lesson was learned: I never again learned my lines in that rigid, inflexible "line reading" manner.

The Active Component of Dialogue

Good actors realize that words are not written simply to express emotion. If emotional release were all that is involved in the effort to speak, that is, if language were simply a short-term release of feeling, people would simply groan, wail, or bark, and guttural sounds would mark the edge of human discourse. The reality is that people release emotion into an array of words to affect other human beings emotionally and intellectually.

Language takes life's human inner emotion to a higher and more functional purpose to convert short-term bursts of emotional energy into long-term functional, logical, instrumentality with the intent to achieve long term goals. Language is the logical, sophisticated, and civilized way to maneuver our external human landscape (other people) to our purposes.

Monologues and Long Speeches

Bad actors often use all the words in the monologue or long speech as one generalized emotional gusher, seeking only to rid themselves quickly of a singular stimulated emotion, rather than encasing that emotion into purposeful logic and language. When they act like that, it has a boring consequence of releasing a whole string of dialogue with the same undifferentiated and re-petitive sound.

Good actors, on the other hand, who learn to convert the many feelings possible during a monologue into the many, specific and differentiated verbal ideas of a script, create a much more inter-esting and varied performance.

Bad actors should consider this: if there were a singular emo-tional source for the whole array of words in a scripted speech or monologue, the mind would just repeat the same line over and over again! Different words (in a speech or monologue … or scene) *a priori* mean different emotional sources behind those differing words; different words, different phrases, and different logical thoughts result from different tactical emotional changes.

Action #2: Large Body Movement

Large body movement, like dialogue and other action, is but an-other goal-seeking, tactical activity, an externalization of feelings organized and overtly manifest to achieve purpose.

However, like dialogue and any other action, large body movement is not necessarily a straightforward, purposeful activity. Movement mirrors life.

People—albeit generally unconsciously—try to obfuscate emotional truth by their movement, just as they try to hide it in their dialogue. A character moves *away* from someone when they are most interested in them, or they move *forward* in spite of panicking and wanting to run away. We lie with our bodies, as well as with our tongues, to achieve our purposes.

There are two kinds of large-body movement: (1) *intent-specific* and (2) *general.*

Intent-specific body movement is movement for practical reasons: getting a drink at the bar, crossing the room to sit in a sofa, placing a towel in the linen closet.

General body movement—which seems at times like random activity, "fidgeting," as it were—occurs because the large amount of emotion the character is feeling at a particular point in the scene impels the character to move in one of two ways: (1) to move toward the other character(s) to express and/or emphasize their feeling—to underline by physical reinforcement, what they are perhaps verbally saying as well—or (2) to move away from someone in order to refract and contain their emotion, hiding it, modulating it, denying its reality in fear that its full expression and revelation would be tactically unproductive.

> *"I'd better move away before I hit someone."*

> *"I better move away from the boss's wife before I kiss her."*

> *"I'd better turn away so the other poker players won't see my eyes too clearly, thus giving them a tactical advantage over me."*

This refracted nature of purposeful general movement usually ends when the emotion is better under control. At that point, the character generally returns to the scene and confronts the adversary head on.

Blocking (or Molding) a Performance

"Blocking" is an acting term that refers to the actor's and director's shaping of an actor's emotion through large body movement on stage or on set.

I remember walking past a men's hat store as a young boy and watching through the window as the hatter made men's felt hats (in those days they were called fedoras). On a shelf above the main counter was a whole array of wooden blocks that conformed to different men's head sizes. I often stood for hours while watching the man making a hat, cutting a piece of rounded flat felt, steaming it to soften it, and then shaping the freshly-moistened felt over the appropriate-sized block of wood; thereby the term "blocking" the hat.

Large body movement blocking occurs when the director (in collaboration with the actor) shapes the moist felt of an actor's emotional life into large body movement. It is similar to the writer shaping her feelings into verbal form, into dialogue. In both creative actions, the actor-as-character's emotions are molded outwardly by the artist/character and expressed into purposeful actions.

Blocking movement can also be characterized as either *organic* (endogenous) or *aesthetic* (exogenous). Organic blocking movement occurs because the actor-as-character feels an inner emotional compulsion to express or contain his emotion in large body movement. Aesthetic blocking, on the other hand, results when the director—as the intermediary between actor-as-character and audience—shapes the actors' movement for symbolic or aesthetic (audience witnessing) reasons: so the audience can best see and hear the actor and be maximally impacted.

Ideally, all blocked movement is dually conceived, with both organic and aesthetic intent occurring simultaneously. To wit, the actor-as-character emotionally feels like moving to a position on stage or on set the director considers exactly the most aesthetically potent.

In any well-blocked scene, whether the large body movement is intent-specifc or general, organic or aesthetic, the dialogue can be stripped from the scene and the movement patterns—established by an actor's emotional urgings and a director's aesthetic sensibilities—become almost as a story-telling dance. The body movement alone reveals the play's or film's conflictual and emotional story.

Action #3: Facial Reactions and Small Body Gestures
Facial reactions, including hand, shoulder, and arm gestures, are small body movements worthy of a separate action category because they are so subtly and quintessentially revealing of human nature. If "the eyes are the windows to the soul," similarly, the face, eyebrows, forehead, mouth, and chin—the frame of the window's eyes—as well as hands and arms (the clenching of fist, the shrug of the shoulders) rank only slightly behind the eyes in revealing a character's personality to the audience.

When I was a young man, my friends and I often took the bus to the New York Port Authority Bus Terminal and stood for hours at the upper exit to the escalators to look down at the faces of the New Jersey to New York commuters riding the escalator.

Standing on high like that, we exchanged judgments on personalities and lives based on the arriving passengers' faces:

Acting is Living

"He's got four kids, hates his job, and is playing around on his wife."

"She is divorced; she's an executive; never been happier."

"She's hot, but poison; I wouldn't want anything to do with her."

With youthful insight, arrogance, and certainty, we used to say, "As you grow older, you get the face you deserve."

Like all actions, facial actions have a purposeful intent and are tactical. While they almost invariably originate unconsciously, these small movements are not passive entities. Rather, they are again active non-verbal statements that attempt—by a turn of mouth, a wink or a glare—to maneuver another character to believe as we believe, in order to get them to give us what we want.

In facial reaction, (1) the face tries to say something—non-verbally—to someone ("That's the dumbest thing I ever heard," or "I love you," or "You really anger me ... and therefore I want you to stop what you're doing that's causing my anger.") to let them know how we feel without actually saying it. In so doing, we try to make them behave in a manner consistent with our needs.

On the other hand, (2) the face often attempts to hide what we feel—in the most extreme case, when we emit a poker face—trying, through a stark obfuscation of feeling, to better achieve an objective vis-à-vis the other character. Audiences can thank God, however, that good actors don't all have excellent poker faces or the audience would never know by facial reaction alone what any character is feeling! A wonderfully expressive actor is really a failed poker face!

The mechanical ability to bring the audience ever closer to an actor's face and body in film and video heightens in importance the value of revealing character through facial reactions and small body movements. With the use of close-ups, the actor's facial reactions—along with small hand and body movements—have become critical, if not dominant, revealers of character truth to the audience.

One of film's classic examples of the power of a close-up is Gloria Swanson's classic line at the end of Billy Wilder's great film *Sunset Boulevard*: "I'm ready for my close-up, Mr. De Mille!" As she approaches the camera, rarely has tragedy's face been so simply, silently, starkly, and so powerfully revealed, the proverbial picture worth a thousand words.

Action #4: Prop Handling

The actor's use of props in any scene can be as vivid and powerful a force in revealing character as any other of the actor's actions. Props can be thought of as extensions of the actor's hands and arms. Like words, body movement, and facial reactions, props externalize and reveal the flow of emotion from the actor-as-character's inner feeling to outer physical action.

In today's world, the prop of a cigarette can reveal to the audience the smoker is a neurotic, addictive, self-destructive personality without the ability to change a counter-productive pattern of behavior. (Of course, fifty years ago the audience would have considered him "cool" and sophisticated ... unless he kept dropping the ashes on the set's best rug!)

A man who taps his pencil impatiently on the desk or holds the phone earpiece away from his ear when talking to his mother-in-law reveals (in his prop-handling) his attitude toward her and the conversation. During a conversation about death, a woman compulsively setting the dishes for dinner or arranging the toolbox reveals the personality profile of someone who is either indifferent to the conversation or someone with a need through indirect action to contain her tumultuous emotion.

The most vivid demonstration of character revelation in on-screen prop-handling occurs in *The Caine Mutiny Court Martial*, starring Humphrey Bogart, whose character, Captain Queeg, is dramatically exposed and destroyed through his unconscious prop utilization during a trial. His whole hyper-manic and guilty personality becomes apparent on the witness stand while he inadvertently clicks—at an increasingly frenetic rhythm—metal balls in his hand while protesting his feigned innocence to the cross-examining lawyer.

Prop Choice

When considering the use of a prop in a scene, the good actor should use the following criteria:

1. *The prop should be logical to context.* No wrist-watches are worn in a shower unless, of course, the script dictates a desire for character absent-mindedness!

2. *The prop should be symbolically revealing* as to character. For example, an anal-compulsive personality wears two watches, stylistically matched, one on each arm.

3. *The prop should be progressively utilized.* An illustration: A man, before going on a date, eagerly selects a watch that color coordinates with his tie and socks. As the scene progresses with his chatterbox date, he becomes bored and refers to the watch constantly. A short time later, during a fight over the restaurant bill, he angrily waves his hand, breaks the watch strap, and shoves the watch into his pocket. During a subsequent and even more heated disputation of the bill,

he sits on the watch, shatters the glass face, and cuts himself. He goes to the bathroom, checks out his punctured bottom, returns to the table, and throws both the watch and the bill at her feet. He exits, then returns, retrieves the broken watch and cries—over the broken watch, but not over her or the bill!

This use of the watch (and, for that matter, the handling of the restaurant bill, another possible prop in the scene) expresses the progression of the scene's conflict and tells the story of the character on a prop level.

The use of props, as well as dialogue, body movement, and facial reactions during a scene, in such a simultaneous and developing progressive manner, makes a scene—in its character revealing possibilities—much more multi-dimensional and dramatically dynamic. The dialogue-issuing, bodily-moving, facially-reacting, and prop-utilizing actor becomes multi-linguistic in the ability to reveal character through multi-action expressiveness.

Action #5: Thinking

When dealing with the action of thinking there are some very important considerations to highlight:

> *People don't want to pause to think; they are almost always forced into it.*

Thinking, properly executed by the good actor, is the body seeking a positive, productive action through the mind's pausing, reflection, absorption and consideration. As such, thinking is often an extremely dramatic moment during which the actor's face and eyes reveal that thinking effort and the often-deep emotional reality behind it. In the action of thinking, the bodily system is stunned for a moment by a newly-arrived stimulus. It requires an extension of time for the new emotion to be absorbed, resolved, and understood before being expressed overtly in the next verbal or outer physical action.

Thinking takes concentrated work, and the audience witnesses the actor's face tensing as the actor-thinker's attention is somewhere other than on their outer reality (in fact, it is inside themselves), often blurring their outer vision. Thinking creates an unfocused softening of pupils, as the actor-as-character attempts to avoid new outer stimuli that could interfere with the internal processing of the prior stimuli.

During that thinking moment, historical costs are being evaluated in some inner-neural cost-benefit analysis. This generally unconsciously experienced delay may take a fraction of a second, or three seconds, or even longer, but during that delayed moment—and this is important to maintaining the active energy in a good actor's performance—the human system works feverishly to think fast, to overcome the delay and come up with a solution.

The ferocity of inner thinking activity makes thinking moments exciting, not dull and static cessations in the flow of the scene. A thinking character is intellectually processing new data, measuring a sensory stimulus against stored data memories, in an effort to get back into overt action mode.

Thinking is an Unconscious Process

Rarely in everyday life are people aware they are thinking because most all thinking occurs sub-cognitively. Because the act of thinking is a spontaneous and unconscious function of the human autonomic system, people are generally too focused on the thinking of the task at hand to be aware they are thinking, per se.

When we are thinking, people ask, "What are you thinking?" to which we honestly respond, "Nothing," or "I don't know." We rarely say, "I am now reflecting, absorbing, and considering before proceeding ... and when I am finished with this inner processing, I will talk."

The Time Needed to Think

The good actor can never really know for sure the amount of time it takes for her feelings to be processed by thinking, much less how long it takes to be manifested in an overt action, because the duration of any thought process occurs in direct relationship to the depth and complexity of true inner turmoil. The actor must, therefore, remember that real thinking is too spontaneous and complex an occurrence to arise in any pre-determined, pre-timed way. The actor may anticipate a thinking moment in a scene, but the usual performance warning pertains in thinking as it does in any other action. In performance, the good actor lets the absorption of real emotion determine the timing of thinking. Trust in this: the audience can and will recognize the rhythm and reality of real thinking ... and will react to the actor's performance positively or negatively accordingly.

Thinking Is a Costly Choice

Generally, people don't want to think. Thought takes effort, and effort is a cost.

The human brain is an evolutionary attempt to transmute the human synapse into a more productive response mechanism. Let's, say, a long time ago, our human ancestors loved to pet animals, affirming "Nice leopard, nice leopard." Over time, repeatedly registering the negative consequences of such an act in our evolutionary DNA, the pet-the-leopard-people were disproportionally eaten and didn't survive long enough to have many offspring. The ones who survived did so because, although they might have liked to pet the soft fur of the leopard, (1) they thought about it, (2) they learned to run away, and, as a consequence, (3) they weren't eaten. The frontal brain of our surviving ancestors grew bigger and able to store away the "don't pet leopards" information.

Even though such evolutionary leaps allow humanity tangibly to dominate the world, they are not cost-free. Human thinking is an investment of time and energy that not only offers the possibility of enhanced future return, but also requires the investment of present costs. The action of thinking is a costly energy claim forced on humans by the challenge of positively surviving their external reality.

> *Actors cannot simply take a thinking moment; they must earn a thinking moment.*

Actors are often erroneously directed or instructed by teachers to "pause and take a thinking moment," to stop, suspend any overt activity, and have a thoughtful look on their face to indicate inner deep emotion. These teachers and directors are wrong in their proposal in two respects: (a) no good actor should ever indicate (show) anything (*indication* is a dirty acting word) by falsely acting a feeling that usually isn't there, or is there and shouldn't be consciously shown, and (b) it is illogical to life. Choosing to "take a moment" is false to life and, therefore, false to good acting. As stated above, thinking is an energy claim forced on—not chosen by—humans by the challenge of external reality.

The actor who desires their character to be thinking at a moment in performance must *justify* the moment. Prior to the thinking moment, the actor must have entered the scene in such an heightened internal/emotional condition that, when he subsequently senses some stimulus in the scene, the stimulus strongly *forces* the actor to pause, carefully consider, evaluate, and sort through options—*to legitimately think*—before commencing to the overt action.

"Taking a Moment": A Valid Rehearsal Technique
Some actors are roadrunners: "beep, beep" … down the road they go! They move so fast toward a scene's goal that they forego any possibility of real stimuli—and real emotional activation —occurring to them. Their rule seems to be to keep moving fast so that life's camera can never get them into focus—and feeling! We often say to such people: "If you'll just slow down, you'll see what I mean," or "Stop and feel," or "Shut up and listen."

As a technique to slow down such roadrunners—to get their emotionally fear-challenged selves to become available to stimuli and resultant feelings—it is often beneficial for the teacher to suggest (in rehearsal or training only) that these actors arbitrarily "take a moment" before saying every line in the scene. Although enforced "taking a moment" is false when used in performance, in rehearsal it forces roadrunners consciously to slow down and become sensorially-available to the external reality in the scene.

However, teachers should suggest this only as a preparation technique used to get such emotionally closed-off actors to look at, listen to, and possibly feel. These actors should not attempt this exercise in performance, however.

Too Many Moments
The excessive use of "moments" in a performance, even when properly justified by stimulus and emotion, can become trivialized by repetition, lose their uniqueness, and become boring. Do you ever talk to someone who pauses and ponders before everything they say, as if they are dispensing god-like pronouncements? Mind-numbing, isn't it?

Acting is Living

If you create too many thinking moments, you wind up with no moments.

The acting term "throwing away" means precisely that: the actor throws away most of the wonderful thinking moments generally gleaned in rehearsal, similar to the suggestion offered to writers that they throw away, in any essay, script, or book, their ten most fondly-felt sentences. Throwing-away means performing some moments as if they were relatively unimportant, rather than fraught with overwhelming significance, which makes the other really important moments the actor experiences in the scene more vivid.

When everything is important, nothing is important. Selective importance in choosing moments enhances the value of the few really important moments in a scene. In acting, as well as in economics, scarcity creates value.

A director friend of mine often tells his actors to operate on-stage as if they were music composers who have limited notes available to use. They are given only two precious half-notes in a scene, and they must reserve those elongated durational moments for the most meaningful passages of the piece. They are given only four quarter notes for the next most meaningful passages. The rest, the bulk of the notes of performance, is comprised of eighth-notes or sixteenth-notes.

To test this thesis, I once asked my good friend and writer, Ron Austin, how many important elongated moments an actor can expect to find in a scene of his. He said "One … and only if I've had good day writing."

Spontaneously generated "moments" are special because (1) they are emotionally meaningful; (2) they are subtlety and quintessentially revealing (about the the character's inner life); and (3) perhaps more importantly, they are rare.

Moments are called moments because they are momentary. The actor should allow a selected few, and then move on.

Special Actions

Character conditions, such as drunkenness, ignorance, and numbness, are special acting actions that involve a unique inner neural blocking mechanism, one in which, similar to thought, the normal sense/feel/action process goes awry. In such special actions, the human system wants to operate normally, but fails; there is an internal block, a complication that interposes itself between feelings and response. The system runs into some internal inhibitor, some internal blockage. As a result, the system is forced to expend extra effort to compensate for the inhibition, and we recognize the inhibiting condition in the extra energy expended to overcome the internal blockage.

In order to perform these special conditions properly, the good actor must—as in all acting actions—first, as she pursues her objective, be stimulated by the external reality, and then allow synapse (emotion) to occur. Next, she must allow any subsequent outer actions to be *delayed*, and that delay, and the subsequent human desire to overcome it, is what is most performance revealing.

The following is an example of the right and wrong way to enact one such action-inhibiting condition: pain.

A bad actor is given a wounded foot to play. He is told to act the pain, so he limps; he groans louder on each step; he scrunches his face severely to indicate how bad the pain is. The director makes the bad acting worse by asking the bad actor to intensify the pain. The bad actor groans more agonizingly when he sets the foot down on the floor and distorts his face even more severely when he takes each step.

A good actor interrupts (he has to!) and says to the bad actor, "You're barking up the wrong tree. Consider what a man does *in reality* when he tries to walk with pain in his foot. He tries to solve the condition of pain, and that action best reveals his painful condition."

The good actor *demonstrates*: he gets off the injured foot, returns the healthy foot to the ground as fast as possible (which is what a limp is), and spends as little time on the injured foot as possible.

Watch yourself next time your foot is in pain. You will quickly put your *uninjured* foot to the ground faster and in direct proportion to the severity of your pain. The more pain, the more quickly the good foot hits the ground, and the greater the limp.

The same dynamic holds true with drunkenness: the attempt at solution reveals the condition. A drunk in reality is someone who tries extra hard to appear sober. The drunk's attempt to act normal—sober—is stymied by the inner inhibitor of an alcohol-numbed motor response (action) system. The drunk tries to compensate for the inhibitor by greater concentration: talking more d-i-s-t-i-n-c-t-l-y when conversing, seeking extra balance before rising from a chair, aiming the body at targets before beginning to walk toward them. The attempt at the solution (in this case, working extra hard trying to appear sober) reveals the inner drunken condition.

The same dynamic holds with a person who has limited intelligence. A flawed neural process serves as an inhibitor to the character's desired normal cognitive understanding. The intelligence-challenged person wants to catch on to things quickly, but can't.

The intelligence-challenged person works extra hard to listen and look to compensate for deficient intellect, and that extra-energetic attempt at solution reveals the condition.

Those who stutter can be similarly analyzed. They are people who try extra, extra hard to talk smoothly, to speak without self-interruption, but an inner inhibitor foils their efforts. Similarly, shy people reveal their shyness by their effort to hide what they feel is their social inadequacy. They avert co-conversationalist's eyes, speak softly, and seem to shrink in posture. They work exceedingly hard to reduce their size and minimize their exposure to (what they assume will be) their inevitable social failures.

In all cases, the attempt at an inhibitor solution reveals the fundamental condition of the character.

Action #00000: The Third Rail of Actions!

There is one action, one possible inner inhibitor, one flaw, one inner blockage that must be avoided at all cost: the actor thinking, or actor processing, during performance. There is no right way to enact that condition properly. An actor who thinks of herself as an actor during performance creates bad acting, period, *a priori*.

The good actor during performance must never extend the normal tri-part nerve cell operation into an erroneous four-part package, allowing their acting to become Purpose→Stimulus→Emotion→*Actor-Self-Awareness*→Action. When that occurs, when the actor imposes in the performance the actor-as-actor's circuit of thought processes—whether the imposition occurs between feeling and action ("I feel; okay, now let me express it") or between stimulus and feeling ("I'm registering a stimulus; oh! I'm feeling it! Now let me act it")—the scene loses its natural flow, the rhythm of reality ... and the audience disengages.

Acting is Living

The good actor must always remember that an actor is hired to live as the actor-as-character, not the actor-as-actor.

The Origins of Human Actions

To emphasize and encourage the good actor to avoid in performance all semblance of actor consciousness, let me state that in everyday life all overt human actions—words, voice and ideas, large body movement, facial reactions, prop handling and thinking—are created by a dual operating system in the human body: the *voluntary* nervous system in concert with the *autonomic* nervous system.

The voluntary system is the portion of our nervous system that is susceptible to conscious control. It creates the grosser motor movements of the human system. I *consciously* choose to lift my arm. I *consciously* decide to move my eyebrows. I *consciously* decide to open my eyelids.

On the other hand, the subtler and more prevalent actions of the human system, the ways eye cells reconfigure themselves in response to differing inner emotional changes, the way the blood flows to the facial tissues when we are angry or embarrassed, the differing sounds of anger in a lover's spat compared to the sounds of anger toward an intrusive, strange third party, all of these more subtle differences in the human response mechanism have their point of origin exclusively in the autonomic nervous system, that part of the human operating system beyond conscious control.

Watch your everyday behavior. See how few times during any twenty-four hour period your actions—movements such as lifting one's arm, raising one's eyebrows, or opening one's eyelids—are produced by your voluntary nervous system, and how few are not. The preponderance of our movement efforts occur on the involuntary, or unconscious, side.

Thus, the bad actor who assigns the creation of his actions to the voluntary system alone ("I will consciously lift my arm and raise my eyebrows, and I will consciously do all of that on stage") rather than in shared coordination with the emotion-driven autonomic (subconscious) nervous system, creates a role with a minimum of human reality. As a result, they bring less than half a human reality to a performance, and the audience will be less than half kinesthetically stimulated (and only by the grosser half at that). Perhaps audiences who view such performances should be charged only half price.

Summary: Reality

Drama is conflict.

Conflict occurs in reality between two or more conglomerates of human nerve cells (human beings) engaged in multiple ongoing stimuli→synapse→response interactions (listening and looking, feeling and resultant actions), organized and energized toward their respective purposes.

In the good actor's preparation, before the scene starts, she activates and heightens the character's past (occurring from prenatal to curtain rise) aided by the application of emotional exercises and techniques that create a destabilized emotional condition in the actor-as-character, an unbalancing of the character's desired emotional homeostasis, which, properly, before performance, settles into the actor's unconscious muscle memory.

In the performance the actor-as-character enters the scene striving for present objectives that she assumes will redress past-created imbalances.

The God of Drama, however, aided by the writer—both being the devils that they are—always create an oppositional reality vis-à-vis that striving, a mutual, conflictual force among character needs.

As the scene progresses all characters, being in conflict, are forced to sense— see, hear, taste, smell and touch—their oppositional external reality as they strive to achieve their purpose, and the sensory data received by the character activates specific emotions drawn from the general emotional reservoir of the character's past.

These stimulated emotions convert—almost simultaneously and almost always by the autonomic system—into specific actions: dialogue, body movement, facial reactions, prop handling, and thinking.

The end result: the audience, through their kinesthetic identification with the specific actions of the actor's overall performance, gets into emotional contact with themselves.

Actors play human beings, and human beings are eye-challenged: they have blurred vision on the past, myopia on the present, and glaucoma on the future.

Chapter 3
Making Sure a Performance is Honest

The third Essential Element of Good Acting, "honesty," is a subset of the need for reality in performance, but it is an acting element often so neglected by the actor—and so important—that I include it as separate category.

An honest performance is one in which an actor-as-character pursues the objective vis-à-vis the other character(s) without any special overriding awareness or insights, past, present or future, into their scripted predicaments. Well-acted characters are like hedge hogs burrowing beneath the soil, only popping up occasionally to discover their whereabouts.

Like people in everyday lives, legitimate characters in conflict, especially those caught up in drama or comedy, have little historical insight into their behavior. They are too engaged in fighting in the present on a moment-to-moment basis toward their goals to have much self-analytical overview.

An honest performance is one wherein an actor lives the life of an unwitting, unaware and unwilling patient; not the life of the wise, omniscient, all-knowing psychiatrist.

Characters are People, Not Gods

In our analysis of "honesty in performance"—as one of the most necessary and important ingredients in good acting—let us first spotlight performance dishonesty in an actor's craft, before moving on some suggested honest correctives.

It is true that actors, in their analysis and rehearsal, should take a god-like perspective of the play/film, viewing the drama from above, as it were, and seeing down onto the overall design of the human tragic-comedy on the page beneath them, to better prepare themselves to subsequently act as characters in the drama. However, these same actors, once in performance, must remember to descend to Earth again, to fulfill their actor-as-character destiny as human beings. Once having analyzed the script from their god-like stance in rehearsal, later they must, as actors-as-characters in performance, live out their drama as Jesus did, no longer as God, but as a God made incarnate, made flesh!

Actors who enter performance and continue to endow their characters with god-like conscious knowledge and insight of the character and script are dishonest actors. They take unfair advantage of their privileged positions as actor-having-read-the-whole-script, insider friends of the writer-god. They are "global positioning satellite-ing" their performances, "playing on top of the material," "playing results," or "end-gaming a performance" (all pejorative acting terms, by the way).

This kind of omniscient acting in performance, taking a God-like perspective while playing a character, is cheating: it is taking a test when you have all the answers. Actors-as-characters who act in this manner are engaging in false, rigged, and dishonest contests. They are "throwing the game," turning the agony of conflict into a "wrasslin' exhibition" ... where knowledge of the outcome is pre-ordained and the contestants are aware of the significance of every move to the overall pre-resolved pattern.

This kind of dishonest acting is, like all other false and unreal acting, audience repelling.

Good actors recognize that comedy and tragedy happen to people who remain blind to their destiny. Comedy and tragedy happen to the innocent, the confident, the unaware, the brave, the unsuspecting, the myopic and the overly-optimistic. Remember: "Fools (and good actors) rush in where angels fear to tread."

Othello had no idea his love for Desdemona would drive him to jealousy and murder. If he had such fore-knowledge, he would never have stopped under Desdemona's window to talk; certainly he would never have chatted, wooed, courted and then married her. Similarly, if Othello had the prescience that Iago was out to destroy him, he never would have called Iago his "faithful lieutenant" and willingly heeded his tragic advice concerning Desdemona and Cassio.

Equally, Oedipus Rex had no idea that he would discover, by his incessant grilling of Tireseus, his own patricidal-past and incestuous-present. If he had, he would have shut up early in Act One and stopped questioning everybody. Tragically, innocently, unwittingly, he played the role of kingly puzzle-solver, and, in so doing, unconsciously created his own demise.

In the beginning of the film *Casablanca*, the character Rick assumes that running a bar in politically neutral Morocco during World War II would be as far removed from his personal involvement in life as he could possibly get. He believed he could spend his remaining years free-floating in the Vichy French Moroccan city, watching others gamble while he safely collected a percentage of their action, distanced from both Axis and Allies, Nazis and Americans, gamblers and lovers, and remain politically and romantically neutral until his dying day. Then: "Of all the gin mills, in all the cities, in all the world, why did she have to walk into mine?"

Comedy and tragedy happen to characters when they least expect it.

Dishonest Elements in Bad Acting

Accordingly, good, honest actors-as-characters must avoid the following performance traits: (1) super cognizance of the relevance and impact of the past on their conflictual present; (2) preternatural awareness of the meaning or symbolic nature of the present; and (3) consciousness of any predictive knowledge about their future.

Memory of the Past

Actors who enter a scene with a constant awareness of the past, the settled mud of their lives, as it were, always at the top of their consciousness, are dishonest actors.

Good actors accept that the past is a very reluctant suitor. Think of how much time and effort psychiatrists normally spend to open up a patient; often it takes years to get the patient to confront their personal past truthfully. And even when actively and logically solicited by personal will (after all, a person chooses to go to the psychiatrist—at an expenditure of $150 an hour or more), the truth remains indoors, buried and swirling deep in the murky bottoms of the patient's psyche. Therefore, an actor who plays his character having—and worse, willing to have—instantaneous, clear, profound insights into the past, especially as it relates to the onstage present, gives a starkly dishonest perfor-mance.

Dialogue About the Past

An honestly-enacted character is generally thrust—dragged kick-ing and screaming—into the past, and most especially a past that produced darker emotions, like sadness, anger, frustration.

When a character is scripted to speak about the past or give a speech or monologue about the past, he must only do so reluc-tantly. Remember: reviewing the past is always an unwilling choice for the character.

One speaks of the past only in order to learn from it, to better operate in the conflictual present, to better achieve the present objective by reviewing, understanding, and relating past events to a conflictual opponent, and thereby to move more successfully through the present, and, hence, into the future. Reviewing the past is a cost of organizing the present in such a way as to (hopefully) ensure a better future.

In everyday life, we delve into the past primarily to learn. ("Those who refuse to heed the lessons of history are doomed to repeat them.") When we finally do confront the past, we re-veal it to others sparingly, and only then out of pragmatic neces-sity and only in an amount sufficient to accomplish the conflictual goal.

The good character-revealing-the-past says in effect: "All right. Here's the truth from my past. It often hurts me to remember it. I would have preferred not to remember it … but because of what you just immediately said or did to me, and in order to achieve my objective, I am forced to recall the often painful past and put it into words as the price of defeating you."

That feature of hesitancy, the character's reluctance to reveal, gives all character speeches about the past their maximum honesty and reality. Talking about the past is like someone having to reach into their wallet to pay the bill: You want the benefits, but only at minimum cost, so you carefully count out the truth one dollar at a time. "Now that you've forced me to deal with the emotional cost of past memories, now that you've forced me to pay that emotional price, I will stay in the game ... I want to divulge it (pay the price of admitted and revealed truth) as quickly and as frugally as possible."

Subtext

Generally what a character is most unwilling to reveal is called subtext. It is a character's hidden emotional history, his genetic inheritance (nature) modified by a lifetime of nurture. It is the buried mud/residual of the character's life, the emotional sum total of his neural inheritances and experiences.

By definition, subtext is buried until it receives kinetic activation by the specific events of a scene, and then surfaces only when activated by those specific conflictual events, and only when the character needs to identify it and use it as a tactic.

Unfortunately, subtext is one of the most commonly used—and, most commonly abused—words in the acting lexicon. When I hear it, I am always reminded of the term "junk bonds," a financial instrument whose market problems caused a great furor in the 1980's.

Junk bonds systemically failed to deliver on their investment promises, and everyone became aghast. Investors asked, "How did junk-bonds turn out to be such a problematic, risky investment?" My response: Why was everyone so surprised? Were investor's ears closed when they bought junk-bonds? *Junk-bonds, by definition, are junk.* What did investors think they were buying: gilt-edged annuities? If these same purchasers had gone to the delicatessen and ordered a "garbage-burger," would they have expected filet mignon between the halves of the sandwich roll?

Bad actors—when they use (and try erroneously to enact) *subtext* —all too often act as junk-bond purchasers: they don't hear the word *subtext.* They act as if they should play subtext on the surface of a performance … which is semantically illogical, of course. Subtext is *sub*; it refers to the emotional truth beneath the text. Subtext is the emotional truth under-girding and pro-pelling an action. As such, it should never be acted overtly at the surface of an actor's performance. It is the sub-textual emotion existing *below* the surface of behavior. This "hidden agenda," as it is often called, is what a character wants, feels, needs, and believes is at his inner operational core, beneath the surface of his behavior. The character's inner life, what's really going on inside the character, is often in contra-distinction of what is going on outside.

The actress Joanne Woodard described a good acting perfor-mance as the peeling of an onion. The core (subtext) of the onion is initially hidden until the blows of plot conflict peel away the onion's outer surface, one layer at a time … until all that is left at the end is a onion's essential core. One can think of this process—this dramatic peeling of personal truth hidden beneath the mask of our everyday deceits and denials—as a four-act paradigm:

The "Lie-Lie" Structure of a Scene (Peeling the Onion)
Act One: Lie/Lie/Lie/Lie. During the first section of a con-flictual scene, I am in a state of denial. I lie to you and I lie to myself about my deepest fundamental emotions (while trying to

achieve my objective through you at the minimum cost of my having to face my personal truth).

Simultaneously, you confront me and lie to me about your deepest fundamental emotions while you try tactically to achieve your objective from me.

After a brief skirmish on these mutually lying terms, nobody wins. The struggle continues.

Act Two: Truth/Lie/Truth/Lie. Tactically we are forced to up the ante: overwhelmed by the force of your tactics, I am forced to discover the truth about me, as you are forced to discover the truth about yourself. However, we both continue to lie to one another. The stand-off remains, but we have started to peel.

Act Three: Truth/Truth/Truth/Truth. Under the duress of your continuing attacks, I am forced to admit my truth about myself to you, and you are finally forced to admit your discovered truth about yourself to me.

We are both unpeeled.

However, in spite of our mutual exchange of tactical truth, neither one has won the conflict!

Act Four: The Deepest Truth/Truth/Truth/Truth. In a final attempt to win, I am forced to discover and reveal to myself my deepest, usually long-hidden truth, the core of my onion, its emotional stem, which I never realized was there. In a final attempt to win, you are forced to discover and reveal the deepest truth to yourself about yourself: your inner onion core.

One of us wins. The other loses. The ending is either happy or sad, dependent on our point-of-view. In either case, the audience wins. It has experienced and learned about themselves ... which is the whole point of the drama.

The Meaningfulness of the Present

Just as bad actors perform dishonestly when they knowingly play the resonance of their past in every action, they are joined by actors improperly acting as if their every onstage action is fraught with present-tense meaningfulness. These bad actors invest each line with the quivering burden of profundity, a vibrato sense of importance, as if their characters are fully cognizant of the universal heaviness of the scene's tragic significance.

Actors whose every onstage action resonates with conscious meaningfulness fly in the face of a fundamental the truth of our everyday life (and, therefore, of good acting): most of us are too busy trying to survive the prose of our present conflictual life to recognize any past or future meaningful dramatic poetry in it.

An example: I drive to work; I assume it is another day in traffic, nothing out of the ordinary. I am listening to talk radio. I certainly have no idea that other drivers who are driving along the various roads with me are in actuality holding my fate in their hands.

However, as we all head toward the same intersection—and a tragic accident—an event in which three of us will die, two will be severely injured, and one will carry a guilty memory of causing the accident until the day he dies, we will all be surprised when the accident occurs. Until then, any meaningfulness the everyday drive had prior to the accident is non-existent.

Soldiers on the front line of battle don't refer to themselves as "grunts" for nothing. The glory, the poetry of battle, is unrealized in the actual moment. It is remembered only fondly perhaps fifty years later ... when a documentary filmmaker records the reminiscing soldiers to reveal how poetically powerful was their military escape from death.

Rosa Parks wasn't trying to start the great Civil Rights movement in America by sitting at the front of the bus. She was just a tired African-American woman returning from work with a sore back and even sorer feet who wanted to sit in the nearest open seat. Poetry may have been her soul, but her prosaic objective was the cushioned seat ... getting off her tired feet and onto her back-side.

Poets are perhaps consciously aware of the present poetry of their lives; philosophers are perhaps aware of the philosophical significance of their everyday events; historians, dramatists, and generals are perhaps aware of the present geopolitical signifi-cance of their presently involved efforts; but to the common soldier, like Rosa Parks—and to most characters in tragedy and comedy—present engagement is not knowingly resonant with meaningfulness. It contains little poetry, philosophy, or history. It is filled with nothing more than mud, blood, and tears, the daily grind of battle ... and the desire for easy and common survival.

Surprise, Discovery and Reversals-of-Fortune
"Surprise" is when something unexpected happens to a charac-ter.

"Discovery" is when the character has a sudden realization of an inner or outer truth, one about which the character has previ-ously been unaware.

"Reversals of fortune" come about when the character expects a particular outcome can be obtained by a certain action, and an opposite condition occurs.

These three elements of unpredictable and unexpected future, the sudden twists and turns of the character's fate, give performing characters wonderful audience-arresting moments of character illumination.

When any bad actor enters a scene with anticipation of the meaningfulness of an event (past, present, and future), it mitigates against surprise, discovery, and reversals, thereby denying the audience these moments of character self-recognition.

To avoid this seductive, bad-acting trap, I often advise actors to set themselves up for a character's "surprise," "discovery," and "reversals of fortune" by remaining, at the beginning of any scene, as ignorant and innocent as logically possible about the past resonance and future implications in any soon-to-be-acted circumstance.

For example: if, at the end of a scene, your character's wife is going to leave you, I advise the actor-as-character to enter his home thinking that he has the greatest of all possible marriages. If the scene is written to make you discover you are a lottery winner, forget at first you even bought a ticket. If the bad guy is going to shoot at you from the basement in a few minutes, enter the scene sure he is on the roof … or even out of town. That way, through innocence and ignorance, desirable dramatic and comedic surprise, discoveries and reversals of fortune are more likely to happen.

Indicating

"Indicating" is another form of dishonest, bad acting. It arises from the bad actor's attempt to show the audience the present meaningfulness of a character's life, rather than simply live it. The actor indicates inner meaningfulness by underscoring with an artificial tone of voice, false verbal emphasis, or body movement that diminish, rather than enhance, the power of an actor's interpretation.

Indicating is a very negative acting term. It is, at its core, bad acting; dishonest acting. It is contrary to life. Most people—and most characters—are rarely aware of the inner truth or meaningfulness of their lives. In those rare instances when they are, they certainly don't want to point out any inner truth in front of the other character with whom they are having a conflictual relationship, especially not someone who is watching them, trying to find chinks in their armor, trying to defeat them. That kind of bad acting is like saying: "Here, other character, look at the deepest truth of whom I am. This is where I am most vulnerable!" It is like waving a red flag at a charging bull.

A suggestion to bad actors who tend to indicate like this is to trust—if you are truly feeling it—that the audience will pick up the meaningfulness of an event without your indicating efforts.

The audience is not stupid: they are very bright, especially in the theater.

The Lie Detector

One of the most egregious forms of an "actor indicating" occurs when the actor who is playing a liar in a scene tries to make sure the audience knows he is lying (once again underestimating the audience's intelligence). The good actor has no need to do that: he can lie honestly, feel the truth sub-textually and lie, confident that the audience will pick up his mendacious effort. Where does that confidence in the audience's perceptiveness come from? The good actor knows that audiences are superb lie detectors.

When a human being lies—let's say, during a criminal lie detector test—the liar invariably exhibits, in the attempt to hold the truth down, a heightened state of blood pressure, pulse, respiration, and other skin conductivity. The lie detector machine's needle goes crazy from that extra effort, and that expenditure of extra energy tips off the machine and the expert using it that the person is lying, holding down the truth, dissembling.

The same blueprint applies when the audience witnesses a lying actor.

Remember earlier, when discussing Stanislavski and his training of actors to play Chekhov, the image of one hand holding down the other hand while attempting to press upward? Do it again: hold your hand out, flat, palm down. It doesn't take much effort, does it? Now place your other hand beneath it, palm up. Push up … hard … against the top hand. Note the greater the lower hand's upward pressure, the greater the effort to hold the upper hand flat.

So it is with a good "lying" actor. When the good actor-as-character feels the inner truth, and holds it down—denies or lies like hell—the truth is still there, always pushing up and susceptible to springing out of the character at any moment. That extra effort to obfuscate the truth is automatically/autonomically reflected in the tension in the liar's voice, in the musculature of the liar's body, and it transfers kinesthetically to the good lie detectors— the audience—who sense the truth in the dissembling act.

Remember: Audiences are practiced liars themselves. They can feel and know (it resides in their muscle memory) the truth beneath the lie. Besides, they have nothing else to do in the theater but watch actors-as-characters onstage! They are brilliant preceptors. Like psychiatrists and other "lie detectors," they are trained to see through the denying obfuscations of a patient.

The good actor knows that the audience can recognize the real hate hidden in the tight smile of an enemy pretending to be a friend, the extra studied casualness in an over-sexed young man trying to convince the girl he doesn't notice her blouse cut halfway to her navel, the confusing look on the face of someone who understands exactly what someone else said—but is trying to convince the other person that he understands nothing.

"Methinks the lady doth protest too much…" is Shakespeare's characterization of the phenomenon involved in lying. The good actor never plays the lie; he just lies and trusts the audience will and can pick up on it.

Dishonest Knowledge of the Future

Acting with dishonest knowledge of the future occurs when the actor-as-character endows the character's performance with an awareness of future events and their emotional import before the event occurs. The two major forms of dishonest knowledge of the future are 1) *anticipation* and 2) *playing result.*

Anticipation

Like indicating, "anticipation" is a negative acting form: bad acting. In anticipation, the actor reacts to another character's lines or other actions before they are even said or done. The actor smiles at a joke before the punch line is delivered, becomes angry before the riposte from the other character occurs, reacts to information that has not yet been revealed on stage.

Anticipation generally occurs when the actor is not really listening to or seeing what is going on in the scene. Instead, the actor is generally "in his own head" during performance, inwardly self-consciously focused on himself as actor, thinking about his own performance and not reacting to the other character's real actions. Or he is perhaps reacting according to some preconceived mental image carried over from the rehearsal process of how the scene could and/or should occur. Or he carries over into the scene (and acts according to) his knowledge of the future scripted events.

In any of these instances of bad acting (of "anticipation"), the other actor in the scene might just as well not be there. The bad actor performs the character actions exactly the same, no matter who or where the opposing actor is!

Playing Result

"Playing result" is another derogatory term for a form of dis-honest acting. Playing result is sometimes called "end gaming" the scene: the actor plays the whole scene feeling at the begin-ning of and throughout the scene the emotional response appro-priate to the end of the scene. He goes through the motions of living out a foregone conclusion; that is, he acts depressed while knowing the girl is going leave at the end, or smiles knowingly throughout the scene because he knows he is going to win the office pool, or trembles at a monster-from-the-deep before it emerges from the slime.

Some Origins of Dishonest Acting

Dishonest acting—hyper-awareness of past, present, or future in the playing out of the events in a scene; indicating, anticipating, playing result—generally results from one of five factors:

1. The actor simply doesn't know any better. Actors often are taught that bad acting (in the forms above) is good acting.

2. Many actors fear the arousal of their own emotional spon-taneity onstage, a sense that if they don't know what is go-ing to happen next, they will possibly "lose emotional

control." To rule out a surprise occurrence, they act as if they (their character) know everything about the scene in advance.

3.   The actor is afraid he won't feel the emotion at the precise moment called for in the script, and that fear causes him to jump the gun, anticipate the emotion, like a nervous sprinter's false start.

4.   The actor chooses to exhibit his acting intelligence to the audience directly—"Let me show you what an insightful actor I am!"—rather than have the audience interpret it through the actor's good acting. Once again, the actor doesn't think the audience is smart enough to figure out what's going on. Therefore, the bad actor thinks the audience needs a poke in the ribs to get the joke or tragic circumstance noted. "You (the audience) will probably miss what's going on, so let me underline by over-acting everything I do."

5.   The actor does not feel any real emotion in the scene, so the actor compensates by pretending to feel. The actor acts/plays the scene according to some emotional choice, underlining it with appropriate vocal and physical emphasis to demonstrate how deeply affecting and moving the moment is (or, rather, would be, if the actor were really feeling it!).

I offer the following list of encouragements to actors to counteract the bad acting tendencies enumerated above to achieve honesty in a scene to mitigate against the seductive sins of dishonest acting, such as indicating, anticipating, and playing result.

1.   Keep your character in the scene stupid for as long as is logically possible (give your character an IQ of 100 or less),

which is what generally occurs when we are operating under great emotional stress, either tragically or comedic. Blood races to heart and groin, away from the brain!

2. Keep your character in as much denial of their reality as your character would be in everyday life (ah, life; that measuring stick again!), psychologically to remain unaware in any of their actions to the implications of past, present, or future "meaningfulness."

3. In performance, have exactly the same amount of knowledge of future events as someone has in everyday life: none.

4. Emphasize to yourself just before entering the scene the importance of pursuing your character's objective and not your own acting efforts. Listen and look at the other character(s) in the scene and respond line by line, moment-by-moment, facial action by facial action, without any knowledge of the future events or any certainty of the other character's possible future behavior.

5. Don't be afraid to lose emotional control in your performance. Just transfer most performance actions to the operation of your autonomic system. Remember, the autonomic system has been safely (up to now) creating, organizing and controlling 99% of your life, and you've survived to this point. Why change things now just because you're acting!

Positive Elements in Good Acting: Creating an Honest Performance

So far, we have discussed many of the elements in a dishonest performance. Now, let us turn the tables and consider positive aspects of an honest performance. What viewpoints can a good actor include in preparation that best ensure their subsequent honest performance? How can the good actor introduce into his performance acting elements that reinforce and perhaps assure his honest acting?

Believing You Can Win

Good and honest actor-as-characters enter a scene confidently, invariably positive about their future success. They refuse to see their foolishness or tragedy coming. They believe they can win with swiftness, ease, and emotional frugality.

Even the most pessimistic of honest characters is win-oriented. They may arm themselves for the possibility of painful defeat by assessing a low probability to success, but once they are "in the game," as it were, they believe they can win! After all, no one enters a game with the dead certainty of—or desire for—defeat. Even a horse trainer who enters a three-legged horse into a race must believe the horse has some chance of winning or else he wouldn't pay the entry price in the first place! An interesting ac-tor-as-character always enters a scene believing he has the ability to convince the other person(s) of his point of view ... and win.

The Honest Capacity to Lose

Each step a character takes in a scene is like walking across a tightrope while fighting the downward pull of gravity. It is an inner and outer balancing act, fraught with oppositional yin or yang possibilities: the desire for success co-mingles with the fear of failure. Good, honestly enacted scenes have neither inevitable winners nor inevitable losers. The good actor enters every scene with neither victory nor defeat certain.

Good actors-as-characters, while wanting to win, have Achilles heels. (The Greek myth of Achilles is found in Homer's *The*

Iliad. It is the story of a God-favored, phenomenally capable and aggressive warrior who has a fatally-flawed, vulnerable heel.)

The good actor must never allow the simultaneous tug-of-war between wanting-to-win and capability-of-losing to create immobilization, or stationary ambivalence, however. That would be like watching a football player carrying the ball, ready to run through the opposing line of scrimmage toward the goal, but because he doesn't want to be tackled, he dances in place, neither moving forward nor backward. (This is similar to the actor, who, at times of a heightened emotional ambivalent choice, pauses forever in seeming prolonged stasis.) When that happens in football, the coach screams, "Head to the line. Find the weakest link in the defense and head toward it. Don't stand there. Do something!" (That should also be said to an ambivalent, overly-static actor.)

The Desire for Easy Victory
People in life want success … easily.

For example, in everyday life we often say: "…If I knew this business, or marriage, or child-rearing, was going to be this hard, I would never have entered into it!" Or, "If I knew how expensive he would be to date, I would never have offered to pick up the first check!" An honest actor (emulating life, once again) enters a scene as if the scene's proverbial road-to-hell is always paved with good, easy intentions. (And he is always surprised at the ensuing bumpiness of the road.) While the honest actor-as-character enters a scene prepared to pay the price demanded to win, he always hopes to spend as little as possible in the quest for victory.

An honest actor walks the optimist's staircase: "One or two more steps and I will be on the roof. One more line of dialogue, one more move across the dance floor, one more short conversation with my opposition and he will easily accede to my wishes. One more lottery ticket ... two at the most ... and the jackpot is mine. Cinderalla thinks: one ball gown, one carriage and two glass slippers, and the prince and I will live happily ever after."

A dishonest actor, on the other hand, enters the scene knowing the scene is going to be arduous and acts that way throughout the scene. He acts as if knows he is going to walk an endless staircase; he knows the odds of winning the lottery are greater than getting hit by lightning.

This dishonest actor-as-character is so burdened with such initial pessimism and misery that the audience soon wonders why the actor-as-character ever entered the scene in the first place ... why he ever went to the bar, or bought the lottery ticket.

The Desire for a Speedy Victory

Honest characters want speedy victories: time is money.

Nobody wants to be stuck in traffic: everyone is in a rush. Everyone wants to be rich, famous and happy ... quickly ... in the proverbial blink of an eye. College students want to graduate tomorrow. They wish one lecture, one semester will lead them to a degree, and earning one BA degree tells them everything they need to know.

Hamlet would prefer to kill the King in Act One; Willy Loman would prefer to make the big sale in Act One; Oedipus would prefer to end the plague in one day; and Ulysses would prefer to get home in less than a week.

The honest actor-as-character obeys this all-too-human desire for prompt victory; he wants to achieve his objective with the first line. He only moves to the second line because the first line fails; and when the second line surprisingly fails, he is sure the third line will bring success; when that surprisingly fails: "All right; one more line ... but I'm sure that one will succeed."

When confronted by a long scene, the character is the most sur-prised and chagrined person in the theater. Long scenes are never by the character's choice (although they may be the actor's choice: they want to stay on stage forever!); long scenes are forced on honest actors-as-characters by the writer.

If a scene is long, it is because the gods of drama have con-spired against the character. Length is never an honest actor's choice. The gods and writers have thrown the plotted storms at the characters, have created innate vulnerabilities that slow the characters' path to victory, sure as Odysseus' susceptibility to pretty women, Hamlet's pension for over-analysis, Willy Loman's fear of old age and job-irrelevancy. Only dishonest actors (and their first cousins, emotional masochists) enter a scene knowing and wanting the scene to be long.

The Desire for a Cheap Victory
(Minimizing the Price of Truth)

A good, honest actor also enters a scene believing he can win as cheaply as possible. A good, honest actor tries to steal a victory, to gain revenue from the other character with as little emotional cost as possible.

A good, honest actor enters a scene like a clever deal-maker. He see himself as a practiced negotiator looking for the greatest possible benefit at the lowest possible emotional price. He acts like a poker player who brings a pocketful of money to the table, but doesn't want to lose any of it.

Feelings, emotions, and truths are painful, unwanted, but often necessary toll fees on the road to victory. The wallet of the honest character may be fat with emotional money, but, in reality, the character is a cheapskate.

An honest actor should enter a scene as if entering an auction. All character bidding (of emotion) starts low, only growing increment-by-increment, as each character's unwillingness to accept defeat drives the emotional bids higher.

My wife found a purse in Utah a few years ago. On it was stitched the inscription: "I'm tired of the search for truth; all I want now is a good illusion." Self-discovery and self-recognition may be part of the victor's laurel wreath, but they are heavy trophies, burdensome spoils of war. Good honest acting always heeds this human truth: characters are forced, dragging and kicking, to discover who and what they are.

A character exhibiting over-eagerness to self-discover their essential reality, to pay the price of truth, is a dishonest actor. That kind of acting is profligate, like a buyer paying a million dollars for a speck of sand, especially when that speck of sand will probably blow back in his eye. Characters want success cheaply. They want to win without cost. Actors who enter scenes overly eager to pay the costly price of emotion and self-recognition are dishonest actors.

Summary: Honesty

Building a Dam; Creating an Honest Structure

Throughout this section on honesty, the actor-as-character has been called upon to be as unaware as possible of the deepest truths of a character's emotions, past, present or future, until emotional revelation is forced onto the actor by the plot exigencies—and when that happens, the characters should only be made to feel and reveal those emotions reluctantly—and only at the appropriately scripted time(s).

Isn't that an impossible acting demand? How can the actor possibly be expected to feel an emotional state throughout the scene, as well as deny it at the same time? Stir up emotions in rehearsal; then, at the beginning of the performance, hide these feelings, only to allow them later in the scene to come up involuntarily to the surface when activated by the specific attack of the conflictual opponent.

What is the good actor: an emotional prestidigitator, a feeling pretzel, double-jointed emotionally in the extreme??!

Yes; the good actor is an amazing construction engineer, a superb emotional dam builder.

The deepest emotional rivers of our everyday lives are generally hidden in reservoirs. They are dammed up behind personal, cemented walls of carefulness, reason, and caution.

When a flow of feeling is released on a daily basis, those deep emotional rivers only pour out carefully through personal small sluices, in manageable, economical, and productive amounts—that is, if we are lucky enough to have personally balanced everyday lives! Therefore, actors-as-characters in a play or film—as living embodiments of everyday life—must act accordingly when releasing their emotion. Good acting is dam building and sluice releasing taken to a more exciting and precise manner.

Cliff Osmond

In rehearsal and preparation, the good actor uses emotional exercises and techniques consistent to subsequent character needs, breaks down a few of their own inner cemented walls, stirs up their personal muddy water, floods their inner selves, deluging the rivers of their own reservoir. This available huge volume of potential character-emotional water is now held in the actor's reservoir, contained just below the flooding level (actors have to continue to live in the everyday world, after all!), but it has been made available for the actor-as-character's use.

Next, the actor sets about constructing a new personal dam: the actor-as-character's dam. The actor utilizes the character's constraints, rather than the actor's own. He builds a newly-formed character profile, cements it with the hesitations, doubts and fears—consistent with the character's conceived personality—to arrange the new, deep reservoir of feelings the actor has prepared (in potential) for the character. This new dam is finely-calibrated, moreover, strong enough to contain the water, but also fragile enough to break apart on cue when the scripted scene demands.

The scene begins. Each characters' conflictual actions batter into the others' dam walls. Soon fissures (appropriate as to size warranted) occur on both sides. Emotional water (emotions in the reservoir) threatens to pour through each character's fissures at increasing rates. When that happens, the characters, like little Dutch boys putting their fingers into the holes of the dike, try to contain the outpouring of emotion by enveloping them in productive words and deeds, encasing these emotions in productive actions—to defeat the other character—to stem the flow.

However, the resultant words, bodies, faces, props—actions—alternately fail, as the mutual conflictual assault continues. More and bigger fissures occur. Both characters are threatened to be flooded.

At the scene's end, as the mutual reservoirs of emotion have increasingly cracked the walls of the respective dams, climax occurs: the dams burst. One character is flooded less than the other; he survives, and wins, while the

other drowns, either comically or tragically. As always, through the ac-
tors-as-characters' efforts, the audience is flooded with the waters of their
own self-recognition.

De-Masking

Another way to look at a good actor's proper preparation for a role is to
view the process as creating and tearing down of personal character masks.

People often "mask" their true faces from one another. They enter a new
situation with their true faces hidden behind a series of stacked masks. The
outermost mask, the dominant—the most comfortably-revealed-in-public
personality, the one we'd like our friends and enemies to see us as—is
offered first. For example, people often say in response to that outer mask,
"She's a sad person." "He's a sexy person." She's an angry person." "She's
an intelligent person."

However, when conflict is engaged, masks are knocked asunder.

If, for example, our outermost mask has been offered as a sad one, it falls
first, perhaps revealing under it a sweet mask. Another blow of conflict and
the sweet mask is lost, revealing an angry mask. Another blow and the
angry mask is ripped off, revealing a confused mask.

Blow-by-blow, the unmasking due to the conflict continues ... until all the
outer layered masks of personality are peeled away, one by one. At the end,
only our true face—the fundamental emotion that guides the character—is
left. We are mask-less ... we have arrived at the penultimate moment of
self-discovery and self-recognition.

The game of tennis is played with two players hitting balls at each other, not two tennis players hitting balls to themselves. Acting and tennis are much alike: they require interdependent activity.

Chapter 4
Making Sure a Performance is Interdependent

Interdependent acting stipulates that each character in a scene must and can only achieve their objective through the other person(s). The other person(s)—and the other person(s) alone—contain the possibility of your character's success in the scene. Therefore, the other character(s) must be engaged, defeated, scored upon, hit with words and deeds, and made to capitulate.

In a boxing match, when two boxers avoid throwing punches at each other while dancing carefully around the ring manifesting little action, but a lot of fancy footwork, referees often say to them: "Make a fight, boys." He places a hand on each boxer's back and maneuvers them actively to engage, to hit each other.

Referees for actors (directors) should do the same.

A good actor should always ask: why is my character in the scene with the other character in the first place; and the other character with me? Both characters could be anywhere else in the world at that particular time; why together? Answer: each character is critical to each other's success. Each character is the absolute primary playing field through which each must move to secure victory. That's why you are there. The other character at that moment controls your character's fate.

Actors who act without an element of interpersonal interdependence in their performances are bad actors. They are like a tennis player manifesting wonderful tennis shots, perhaps brilliant lobs, cross-court shots and volleys, but, in reality, only hitting the ball off a high brick wall between herself and the opponent. In such cases, each player indulges in a non-interdependent activity, isolated in her own world, the game narcissistically played between herself and herself. Imagine two basketball teams on opposite sides of the court playing a half-court game of basketball among each other, but never crossing the center line to engage the other team. The crowd would encourage one team to engage the other team, to move the ball through the other team's defense to score goals in the other team's basket.

Crying Uncle

As neighborhood kids we used to wrestle in the park. We'd tumble energetically on the grass or in the cement alleyways of the old apartment building across the street. On rainy days we'd even wrestle indoors on our mother's favorite couch! I vividly remember the tenacity of each engagement: throwing my opponent onto the ground or carpet, pinning his arms painfully behind his back, while tears streamed down his face, me pressing his face hard on the wrestling surface.

Sometimes he would delay, squirm, cry and groan in defiance, without admitting defeat. When her sister was present, she would be mad at me for hurting him, but my opponent would tell her to be quiet: he knew the rules of the game. He knew how important it was for the conqueror to force the vanquished to admit defeat. I'd twist again. Only when he said the words, "you win ... uncle!" would I let go. (And if the tone of "uncle" wasn't convincing, I continued twisting the arm until he convinced me I had won.)

In good acting, there is no back-door escape from the need for interdependent conflict, there is no way for the characters to escape the essential engagement or confrontation with the other person. The other character(s) must be dealt with until she overtly admits defeat. "I'm right, you're wrong," the good-actor, arm-twisting opponent says. "Admit it."

Moreover, that final admission of defeat by one or the other character—the true cry of "uncle"—can only occur at the end of the scene. If there is more writing on the page, dialogue to be delivered, the scene cannot be over. All admissions in a scene of defeat by any character prior to the end of the scene are tactical attempts to disarm an opponent. True and final admissions of defeat can only occur at the end of the scene.

Interdependent Monologues and Soliloquies

Monologues and soliloquies, even when seemingly operating alone, are interdependent acting, interdependent conflicts working toward and through someone or something else. A monologue (or soliloquy) can often be viewed as a dialogue between two people: one real and one imaginary. Sometimes the solitary speaker is split into two: her inner ego is in serious opposition to an alter ego—each side of her engaged in an interdependent argument to resolve a inner dilemma.

Monologues are so named because only the verbal side of the conflictual equation is provided by the writer. In Greek (Western drama's beginnings, remember), *mono* means "one," and *logos* translates as "words," so, *one speaker of words*: a monologue. However, the good actor always understands that a monologue is still in reality a dialogue, a moment-to-moment interchange of interdependent points of view between two independent bodies of opinion, two interdependent sides of us, whether imaginary or inner, creating a conflictual exchange of verbal and non-verbal responses.

For example, in Hamlet's famous "To be or not to be…" soliloquy, one side of Hamlet, the active side, tries interdependently to convince (defeat) his other side, the reluctant-to-kill-the-king side of him. Hamlet Side #1 wants Hamlet Side #2 to kill the king, as ordered by his ghostly father. On the other hand, Hamlet Side #2 wants Hamlet Side #1 to desist from taking the revenge-taking action.

They argue back and forth, each side issuing to each other contrary sets of conflicting ideas-as-arguments: "To be…," says Side #1. "…or not to be," the other side instantly avers. "Whether to suffer the slings and arrows of outrageous fortune…," Side #1 proposes. "Or to bear them…," the other side counters. "To sleep…," Side #1 side wishes. "Perchance to dream…," the other side warns. "Ay, there's the rub…,' Side #1 admits.

And so it goes, throughout the speech: one character; two voices; both Hamlets. The entire play depends upon which side of Hamlet will win: the ego or the alter ego; the would-be killer, the son, or the philosophical pacifist, the student? Will Hamlet Side #1 convince Hamlet Side #2 to kill the king, or vice-versa, will Hamlet Side #2 convince Hamlet Side #1 to desist? Hamlet is an intellectual schizophrenic: two inner voices arguing aloud with one another while trying to resolve the inner conflict.

Relationships as Interdependence

"Relationships" is an acting term for the need for human inter-dependence given either an historical context or a present objective-related context.

The historical context first: the word relationship derives from the word *relate*, which comes from the Latin word meaning "to carry back" (hence, the historical sense).

When actors are asked to analyze a scene, they often say the most important element in a scene is the character's *relationships*. By that they usually mean they must prepare to operate through the other characters in a scene in a manner consistent and logical to their prior history with those characters: husband to wife, brother to sister, worker to boss, friend to friend. In this sense the word reminds actors that, in order to ensure emotional logic in a scene, characters must interact with one another based on their emotional past/history, and that these emotional shadings must logically be manifest in performance.

However, the word relationship has a secondary meaning as well: "to tell," to *relate* (in the present sense).

In the present-tense sense of the word, a character relates to others in the scene (in the sense of "tell them") based on ob-jectives, on what each character needs from the other now. "I re-late to them, I speak and gesture to them in words and movements according to what my present needs are."

In this present-tense use of the word relationship, present needs often trump past emotions.

For example: it's amazing how a lifetime of hate for my father (due to the past) can turn into instant love (in the present) when

Cliff Osmond

I want and receive $10,000 from him to pay my debts. Or how much my fondness for my best friend (due to the past) turns into anger (in the present) when she betrays a confidence. Or an impersonal business relationship (based on the past) can turn sexual (in the present) when I walk into my sales partner's hotel room for a business meeting and she is waiting for me, undressed, and in bed.

The legendary Hollywood producer and studio head Samuel Goldwyn was furious at a studio-contracted writer (I'm sure it had to with the writer wanting more money). Goldwyn flew into a towering rage and refused to even talk to the offending writer; in fact, he ordered an underling to throw the writer off the studio lot. A week later, from his office window, he saw the writer still on the lot. Goldwyn, feeling more furious than ever, gestured to the accompanying assistant: he screamed, ranted, and raged at the underling, and told the underling to get that writer off the lot.

"What should I say to him," the underling asked?

"Tell him I never want to see him again ... unless I need him!"

A performance relationship enacted solely on the past is about as interesting to watch as two people with a faraway gaze, thinking back to a time when they were in love. (Try spending two hours with two people like that, fixed exclusively on the past, ruminating on old love, whether on stage or in everyday life, and you soon discover how limited that can become.) What makes revisiting old love much more interesting is wondering, "Will those two people once again get together ... now ... in the present?!"

When a father and son enter a scene with a history of hate and violence, what is more fascinating is how they got to this state of

animosity, or what they are going to do with each other now, -
the present, and, even more so, finding out why have they come
together in the scene to talk. What do they want from each
other? How will that work out?

Static, expository acting of past relationships that lack an admix-
ture of present objectives and conflict (and emotions) is not
overly dramatic. When two characters are linked only in terms of
the past, their performance will, by definition, be partially dead,
over, lifeless, mere analytical essays of yesterday; obituaries, if
you will.

The active interdependence of present goal-seeking objectives is
what gives past relationships their most dynamic, living, emotional energy.

Beware the Solitude of Rehearsal

Solitary rehearsal is one of the great toxins to good inter-de-
pendent acting. In sole rehearsals, mainly through endless repetition, actors often create an isolated performance mode, and by
the time the scene starts on stage or on set, they are operating
alone, as if in a glass bell jar. They have already decided in rehearsal not only what they are going to say (the learned
dialogue), but also how they are going to say it, irrespective of
the in-performance reality of the other character(s) in the scene.

The opposing character could be a mummy or a mannequin because the over-rehearsed actor would still act and re-act to them
the same way!

As an antidote to just such over-rehearsal-induced, non-interdependent acting, I suggest the following: while standing in the
wings or just before the camera rolls, waiting for the scene to

commence, the well-rehearsed actor really looks at the other actors with whom she will play the scene. I mean, really looks at their faces, the way the light bounces off their hair, the slope of their shoulders, the texture of their skin. See in the other actors something you have not seen in them before: the mole on his cheek, the way he smiles or breathes. In that manner, you can make other actors you are about to act with new, fresh to you again.

Then, just before entering the scene, commit yourself to attaining the character's objective through that actual person in the wings opposite you, including their newly-discovered moles, hair, smile, shoulders and all.

Michael Shurtleff, in his excellent book *Audition*, proposes as one of his "Guideposts" for improving an actor's performance: "Put love in the scene," offering it as an effective method to inculcate in actors a sense of interdependence. His argument is that by forcing yourself to love the opposing character in a scene (even a killer), it makes your actor-as-character vulnerable to the other character, makes your actor-as-character beholden to the other characters' good graces and desirous of their agreement, thereby building aspects of character interdependence. Caring about someone, even an enemy, heightens the interdependence factor of any conflict.

The Meisner Technique: Training Acting Interdependence

In the early days of the second half of the Twentieth Century, when the Stanislavski method of acting training was the craze, no American teacher of the "The Method" was hotter than Lee

Strasberg, initially out of New York's Group Theater of the 1930's (and, after that, the Actor's Studio).

Strasberg, along with Stella Adler, Sanford Meisner, Uta Hagen and her husband, Herbert Berghof, among others, utilized Stanislavski's psychology-based acting techniques and exercises as "emotional recall," "substitution," "given circumstances," "sense memory," "repetition exercises," and the like … all brilliantly popularized in America as the Stanislavski-born "Method" of actor's training.

Strasberg's teaching emphasis, similar to his predecessor Stanislavski, was to hone in on and explore the personal and private details of an actor's own life, to foment within the actor emotional essences drawn from the actor's own personal experiences, so that subsequently the actor could draw on those personal essences to prepare a particular role in a deeply emotional and lifelike manner.

His colleague Adler, on the other hand, emphasized the actor concentrate on the "given circumstances of the play," to therein find the essential performance truth of a character. Uta Hagen, another of Strasberg's colleagues, underscored "substitution" as an emotional technique (the process of substituting an event from one's own life to personalize the character's experience), while Meisner focused on a series of "repetition exercises" to induce and strengthen performance interconnectedness, openness, and sense of reality.

All these teachers were successful. All had their adherents and their detractors. But, adherents and detractors alike would concur that these teachers were similar in focusing where the proper target the actor-in-training arrow should be aimed: emotional honesty and reality. They disagreed only on the most efficient training vehicle to carry the actor there.

Strasberg and his approach initially became the most noted; his emphasis on personal emotional stimulation through private personal emotional exercises seemed to fit the timbre of his time best, to catch most effectively the common mood and the needs of his generation of actors.

The 1940s and the early 1950s in America were considered, perhaps not unfairly, a time of emotional reserve and repression: *Ozzie and Harriet*, *Leave It to Beaver*, backyard barbeques, crinoline skirts, and Norman Rockwell. The unsettling emotional tumult of the Depression (1930s) and World War II (early 1940s) were behind, and America looked forward to relaxing and enjoying life. Small town America became and was captured, photographed, and dramatized as going to the bowling alley, eating out at the local diner, enjoying the latest film at the drive-in or local movie theater, and attending church/mass on a Sunday morning. (By the way: when is the last time you saw anybody in a contemporary movie or play go to church on a Sunday morning or any other day, for that matter … except to get married or attend a funeral?)

Most actors, like most artists in any generation, tend to be rebels, and rebels-in-acting-training are also creatures of their time, even in their rebellion. The would-be actor-rebels in the 1940s and 1950s came from the same placid homes as many of their manicured brethren: Des Moines, Los Angeles (the San Fernando Valley), Grand Rapids, small-town Texas. Once having arrived in major theatrical cities, like New York and Hollywood, they yearned (as rebels) for the anti-repression exercises and emotion-freeing techniques of The Method to rid them of their small town societal and personal constraints.

Actors, such as Marlon Brando, James Dean, Montgomery Clift, Geraldine Page and their student colleagues, newly-arrived in New York, sought out teachers to train them for the new emotional combustibility underlying the work of such playwrights as Eugene O'Neill, Arthur Miller, and especially Tennessee Williams, with his brilliant exposure of the repressed Southern fury and passion that under-scored gender, race, culture, age, and sexual orientation.

To fulfill their desires, the Actor's Studio, Neighborhood Playhouse, and HB Studios, among others, became the chosen places to study, and the teachers, such as Stella Adler, Uta Hagen, Stanley Meisner, and especially Lee Strasberg, fit the actors' emotion-rebellious desires like a glove.

As a result, and in great measure due to the collaborative and energetic effort of all these actors, writers, directors, and teachers of the new emotional/psychological realism, the placid stage and film fantasies of the 1950s gave way to the emotionally explosive content of the 1960s/1970s/1980s. Freed-up emotion presented itself everywhere: in acting classes, in the movies, in the culture. Romanticism, passion, a kind of emotional revolution filled the air—and the airwaves. Strasberg and others like him (in and out of acting) created an emotional rebellion.

Life has a way of twisting and turning. The pendulum swings.

"Do your own thing," the rallying cry of the following highly freed-up generation, the 1960s and 1970s generation, soon degenerated into the scream of actor self-centeredness of the 1980s and 1990s. Society seemed increasingly to back off from a modern Copernican world, where the earth's the solar system and our place in it is just one system among many, and returned to an older Ptolemaic universe, where the universe revolves around the earth, and, most especially, around me. Actors—and society in general—had become so much in contact with themselves and their emotions that they seemed to have lost contact with each other. Alienation, self-interest, psychological fragmentation—both personal and societal—ruled the day. America became a personalized Yugoslavia: Balkanized—rife for disintegration. (To be fair, the freed emotional life led to the great benefits for many during that period: multi-culturalism, gender and racial equality, diversity; positive—long overdue—social changes swept through the American fabric.)

But diversity often creates divisiveness. While we became in those decades into deep contact with our inner child, we often couldn't stand anybody else's children: "Shut the brat up; I can't hear myself scream!"

As a result, the newer generation of hungry actors who came to New York were from that newer, freer, and more self-oriented American context of the 1960s/1970s/1980s, but ironically found themselves more personally isolated. Touching became invading someone else's space, rather than an attempt at personal emotional intimacy. For this newest generation of actors, "interacting with others" all too often meant pressing a key on their personal control panel, having a "colloquy with myself," while not looking and talking with another living sensory person.

TV shows about dysfunctional and alienated families started to (and still do) rule the airwaves. We strove to achieve personal connection in a world of soaring divorce rates, a post-modernist creed of subjectivity, an isolated sense of self and truth, an alienation from Cartesian objectivity rushing headlong into postmodern Einsteinium subjectivity. Classic TV comedy became filled with thirty- to forty-year-old dysfunctional single men and women trying to find any social unit, usually failing amidst a neurotic chuckle and a canned laugh track.

These newer actors, unlike their brethren in the 1940s and 1950s, found their personal emotion easier (too easy, in fact) to access. They also found themselves increasingly achieving their emotional freedom through unappealing self-inducement and self-activation, moving the source of their emotional stimulation from other to self. Accordingly, the Strasberg center of attention, with its emphasis on individual emotional experiencing, began to give way to Meisner's teachings and his focus on human interrelating as a touchstone of feeling. "The Method" soon became a pejorative term for acting self-indulgence, and the emphasis of Strasberg's (and Stanislavski's) teaching methodological faded.

As a corollary, the popularity of Meisner's teaching, with its focus on being in strong personal contact with a scene partner, grew enormously. His methodology became all the rage, with its emphasis on "repetition exercises," looking and listening to a partner in an exercise over and over and over and over again. (His formal program: two years of repeating what someone else says to you, what someone else does to you—and repeating it back to make sure you are really looking and listening—before you can even start formally working a written scene, became popularized.) Actors were now learning again to focus on looking and listening, learning how to come into contact with a world outside themselves, to focus on emotion not as a thing in itself, but as a byproduct of you and me ... to interact ... to interface ... not with a computer or a TV set, but with each other.

The new Meisner training became a form of Mao behavioral modification: the corrupted over-emotional bourgeois actor (the 80s and 90s kind) was sent to the interactive playing fields to learn interdependence and other-reliance. The learning chant became: "there is a world outside you ... there is a world outside you ... there is a world outside you ... look and listen ... look and listen ... look and listen," and became the newest acting mantra.

In this manner, modern American acting—and the element of acting interdependence—found its most recent teaching guru in Meisner

Stanislavski, the great Russian actor, teacher, director and theorist, said that good acting is "being private in public." As a corollary, I offer that the good actor must learn how to perform privately-in-public so that audiences can witness publicly-in-private.

Chapter 5
Making Sure a Performance is Witnessed

Many years ago I worked on a film called *Oklahoma Crude*, starring George C. Scott, Faye Dunaway and John Mills. The producer/director was Stanley Kramer. The 60-person company was ensconced in Stockton, California shooting a scene where John Mills, playing Faye Dunaway's father, was to fall off a high oil derrick and "die." The shot was arranged by director Kramer so the camera would capture the profound shock and grief that Miss Dunaway was scripted to exhibit at the sight of her father's death. Right after Mr. Mills (the stuntman, of course) hit the ground, Ms. Dunaway, on cue, was directed to move from the door of her cabin to the oil pool in which he was marked to play dead and deliver her lines of dialogue.

Not wanting to inhibit her emotional performance within narrow blocking confines, Mr. Kramer and his cinematographer, Bruce Surtees, set up the filming with abundant room for Miss Dunaway to vent her grief. The camera was mounted on a dolly track in front of the cabin door, with the track extending toward the place where the body would fall.

"Feel free, Faye, experience," Mr. Kramer told Ms. Dunaway. "Do not worry about the camera." He assured her that wherever she moved—between cabin doors to the fallen body—the camera would follow her.

The camera rolled, Mr. Kramer yelled "Action!" and the stunt man tumbled a hundred feet into the air bag. A perfect stunt; Mr. Kramer was delighted. As John Mills (replacing the stunt-man) lay "dead" in a nearby pool of oil off-camera, the camera panned to Ms. Dunaway. She exited the cabin on cue. She saw her father dead on the ground, moved toward him, and knelt a moment near his prostrate body. The camera zoomed in to a close-up to catch her grief … but Ms. Dunaway, before delivering her dialogue, suddenly rose and walked away behind the cabin—and out of view of the camera.

The camera kept rolling. Everyone waited for Ms. Dunaway to return to camera visibility. Ten seconds passed, twenty, thirty. George Scott, her co-star, who had been directed to move into the scene to share her grief, stared.

Scott stared at the cinematographer. He stared at Mr. Kramer. He stared at the cabin. The whole cast and crew stared and waited. After two minutes, Mr. Scott walked to his dressing room. Ms. Dunaway never reappeared. Finally, Mr. Kramer yelled "Cut!"

Mr. Kramer was not happy. The whole oil derrick stunt would have to be set up and executed again. Stanley gave the crew his instructions, and then moved to Ms. Dunaway, who finally emerged from behind the cabin.

"Faye … what happened? Where the hell were you?"

She looked innocently at him. She seemed surprised that he was annoyed. "You said to move wherever my emotion made me feel like moving. My feelings wanted me to be alone, not to be seen by anyone, to mourn in private."

Actors act so audiences can witness. Berkeley's philosophical conundrum applies: "Can a tree be said to fall in the forest if no one hears it?" Actors, directors, sound people, camera people, and lighting people are paid to heed this fundamental need of audiences to see, hear, and experience—i.e., to enable the audience to witness—the actor's performance.

The Actor's Need for a Good Vocal Instrument

Because words are so central to an actor's performance—especially in theater, where the spoken word is the primary vehicle of emotional life of a character—the actor needs to have a highly developed, albeit often subtle, responsive verbal mechanism, which includes a well-developed brain (dialogue/words = logic!) to reflect the complexity of any character's emotional experience.

Without a fluid and profound physical/intellectual instrument, actors are destined to live lives of limited discourse. Actors who are intellectually challenged like that are like thinkers with a million ideas, but restricted to hundred word vocabularies. How sad if an actor is able to understand and feel the complex feelings of a Shakespearean character—and eager to reveal that complexity in performance—but has not developed the breathing capabilities, intellectual capabilities, or elocution abilities to serve the verbal demands of Shakespearean discourse. How sad if, in the middle of a character's inner dramatic war (such as Shakespeare always gives us), an actor's performance, while possessing emotions equivalent to an advanced nuclear bomb, lacks the missile system (the body and mind) to deliver it effectively. Without such developed ability to speak (and move) with power and expressiveness, an actor is sadly limited.

Even in film, where the verbal and physical blocking demands are seemingly less rigorous, highly-developed bodily workings are essential. (Sometimes small paintings are more craft-demanding than large canvases.)

That is why acting training—for both film and theater—consists of speech classes, singing lessons, articulation exercises, breath and vocal projection techniques, and why beginning actors, early in their training, are asked to play a tree, cavort like a panther, or climb an imaginary building, all in the service of developing their entire physical system. Only a freed and subtly developed vocal and bodily instrument can freely express and reveal, with precision and power, the deepest and most complex of emotionally dramatic human truths ... for which the good actor always strives ... whether on stage or onscreen.

Strengthening Vocal Power

There are some actors, however, who cannot—try as they might —speak with power. I am not necessarily talking about loudness or tone here. They seemed cursed with weak voices. Their voice seems to have no intrinsic "weight"; it sounds "thin," reed-like.

Am I suggesting that such actors are doomed to a career of verbal non-sufficiency? No. Breath control, not genetically inherited vocal inadequacy per se, is often the issue (an insufficient breathing/vocal symptom caused by tension). Instruction in proper breathing and relaxation techniques with a vocal coach is strongly recommended for all such thin-voiced actors.

I also sometimes recommend such thin-voiced actors go home and stand up against a wall, shoulders flush with the wall, and practice shouting … but without moving the shoulders from the wall (without "pushing" the verbal arrow, if you will).

It will be hard at first. The shoulders want to leave the wall, the chest wants to constrict and move the vocal effort forward, but practice will make perfect. With such practice, everyday voices will gradually take on more depth and weight.

I also recommend to such actors that they—while still speaking with shoulders against the wall—think of having a mouth drawn on their abdomen. They should learn to speak from that lower abdominal "mouth" because when one speaks from the abdomen and the diaphragm, the chest is forced to relax. There is less tightening of the vocal mechanism, the cause of a "thin voice," since proper vocal power is now appropriately centered in the diaphragm, not a tensed chest. With such practice, the thin, reed-like voice often disappears and the voice takes on a proper weight and resonance, a forceful timbre.

Technical vs. Mechanical

The ability of an actor to manage vocal, bodily, and all other good acting witnessing requirements is often called "having good technique," an appellation generally considered by actors to be a compliment. Being a good technical actor means an actor can maneuver his way smoothly and spontaneously through theater's and film's audience witnessing demands.

However, sometimes the term "technique actor" becomes a back-handed compliment, a mild, sneering, subtle critique. Being a technical actor means you have excellent mechanical physical acting skills, but no organic—emotional—acting skills. You are a virtuoso in fulfilling the external witnessing demands of acting, but in so doing, you provide non-spontaneously dead performances ... performances devoid of any emotional reality.

As a result, I advise an actor, when navigating the dual shoals of witnessing requirements and the need at the same time for an actor to create a live, exciting performance (one worth witnessing), think of the word "mechanical" in place of "technical." I believe ALL good acting is fundamentally technical; all good acting involves the *technique* of wedding inner emotion with outer expressiveness. Technique is nothing more than the application of cause and effect— "Do this and that will happen"—at such a high level of probability that it takes on a machine-like, or technical, aura. A good *technical* actor (as opposed to, in my terms, a mere *mechanical* actor) means one who makes his excellent inner emotional technique co-join with excellent outer mechanical technique, the result being overall (and excellent) *acting technique.*

"Mechanics" are the voice, body, props and other performance elements of form preliminarily stripped of their inner emotional urgencies. They are—as I have referred to in another section of the book—the activities of the voluntary nervous system (for example, "I lift my arm because I choose consciously to lift my arm"), rather than actions emotionally dictated by the autonomic system.

When I say to an actor, "Let's get the 'mechanical' challenges of your performance out of the way first," I am referring only to outer physical adjustments irrespective of inner emotional origins. "You inverted words in the third line. You forgot to pick up the glass at the end of the scene. Talk louder; I couldn't hear you in the middle of the scene. I need more 'pace' in the beginning." Of course, when I make such cryptic external mechanical demands on an actor, I assume the good actor of course knows that all the outer mechanical forms must ultimately be created in his final performance with inner true emotional urgency.

A final prompting to actors with reference to external physical mechanical demands: too many young actors—and directors—get so caught up in the mechanics of acting, organizing the physical place settings, that they forget to cook the meal. Even the most beautifully-appointed restaurants (actors) can't stay open long if they serve a lousy (unreal) meal.

Mechanical acting without real feeling is like giving birth to a beautiful baby: a dead one. Fulfilling witnessing requirements must never negate emotional performance requirements; in any good performance, emotional technique and mechanical technique must always be symbiotically joined into overall good acting technique.

Theater Acting versus Film/Video Acting

"What is the difference between theater and film/video acting? Are there witnessing requirements between the two media that create any qualitative differences in an actor's performance?"

Those questions are asked by almost every young actor I confront, and I invariably tell them the difference between theater and film is much less complicated than most are led to believe. Simply put, the difference is purely quantitative, not qualitative; it has to do only with the placement of the audience.

In theater, the witnessing audience is fixed in their seats, generally some distance removed from the performances, whereas in film and video, the audience is almost infinitely mobile ... and that *distance-quantitative fact* is the central, crucial, and sole per-

Cliff Osmond

formance-effecting difference between the acting demands in the two media!

Think of it this way: the theater audience-member is stuck in Aisle NN, Seat 23, whereas the film/video audience can be moved by the director along an almost infinitely flexible continuum of time and space. Film and video audiences can be shipped instantaneously to a satellite circling the earth or up close to inside the eyeball of the actor; from Rome in the year 2045 to Augustus Caesar' time in Year 1 of the Common Era; from Des Moines today to New York, Jakarta, or Mexico City tomorrow, all in a fraction of a second.

Therefore, performance demands and their necessary response differences between theater acting and film/video acting, as well as differences between scriptwriting and playwriting, emphases in actor training, as well as other differential factors between the two genres, such as the grossness or refinement in painting a set or applying makeup, can be viewed from that single effecting source: the relative distance and mobility of the audience between the one media and the other!

When good actors work in theater, they should think of themselves as visiting with Great Aunt and Great Uncle, who are partially sighted and partially hearing (a theater audience). When an actor performs in Auntie's and Uncle's presence (in the theater), the actor must speak louder ("project") and move more boldly to facilitate Uncle's and Auntie's faulty receptivity, just like when going to visit their real life aurally- and visually-challenged older folks.

However, when those same actors return to the set to act in a film or a video, they should accept that Auntie and Uncle have been magically transformed—by camera and auditory equipment

—into impeccable listening and looking machines. Those film and video actors can just talk and move with everyday normality again!

An important reminder to good actors, however: the fundamentals of good acting must always be present whatever the venue and whatever the actor's need to adjust their performance size. The ten essential elements of acting—most especially the ever-present demand for emotional reality: acting truth—must always apply. Just, hopefully, as in everyday life—and this is especially critical to remember for the actor who over-worries about their projection in theater—a good niece or nephew must never act falsely in front of Great Aunt and Great Uncle just because the old folks can't see and hear very well.

(A FINAL NOTE in this regard: the good theater actor must also remember that all hearing- and sight-challenged Aunties and Uncles are not the same: the audience needs vary in their personal "challenges" and, thus, require differing actor adjustments. Specifically, no "one-size-projection-fits-all." Proper projection in theater vastly differs in a 3000-seat auditorium versus a 99-seat theater. Other than that, however, whether in large theater or small, in theater acting or in film/video acting, always obey the ten elements of successful acting, and don't change the essential truth and excitement of what you are saying.)

Q&A: Witnessing Requirements of Theater versus Film

Q: *"The film actor has only 'a rehearsal or two' before having to 'shoot,' whereas in theater, the stage actor is granted up to six weeks of rehearsal before opening night. Doesn't that create an important difference between theater acting and film acting?"*

Cliff Osmond

A: No. There is more in common in these seeming differences than meets the eye. For example, the difference in rehearsal time can be explained by several factors:

1. Consider: film actors do rehearse a lot—on camera. All rejected pieces of film, or "takes," are in effect rehearsals! So although film actors get less continuous "pre-opening night" rehearsal time, over the length of a production film/video actors probably rehearse as much on film/tape as theater actors do on stage.

2. Another reason for the difference in rehearsal time between the two media lies in the different length of subsequent performance demands. For film actors, line memorization —and emotional preparation—for tomorrow's filming (for perhaps only two pages of the whole script) are all that is required in one sitting.

3. In theater, on the other hand, the stage actor is given more time to rehearse prior to performance because in theater the actor is obliged to present in their performance the totality of dialogue, all the lines, the timing, and the sequencing of the total character development for a continuous two hours.

Q: *"A theater script is more verbal than a film script. There is more dialogue. Does that signify an essential difference?"*

A: No. Dialogue is the primary vehicle of the drama in theater because of a quantitative consideration once again: the audience is too far away to distinguish fully the actor's subtle non-verbal "language" of facial and prop-handling actions. Therefore, dialogue language has to carry a far greater burden of the kinesthetic transferal responsibility. There is an old saw: "In novels, characters think; in film, they do; in plays, they say."

On the other hand, to balance the equation, in film/video, since there are more "close-ups" (aiding in audience proximity), less has to be verbally said. "A picture on film is worth a thousand words."

Q: *"Physical movement seems to be more important in theater rather than film."*

A: In film, the camera (and therefore the "image" of the actor through cutting) rather than the actor himself, is constantly moving, expanding and diminishing the actor's impact; whereas in theater, where the audience and the actor(s) on stage are relatively fixed, the actor often has to assume that burden (and opportunity) of creating impact through movement.

Interestingly enough, theater actors often complain that they feel physically shackled when acting in a film, especially when doing "close-up." They feel they have wasted years of a creative theater actor's movement classes, dance lessons, and mime to stand, now in film, in one spot in a close-up and deliver many lines.

I empathize with them, but remind them that in close-ups, the subtle movement of the eyes, hands, shoulders, and brows are body movements, too. They require equal grace, strength and fluidity ... and that those dance and movement classes have more often than not have provided "freeing-up" help in that regard.

Think of it this way: in theater, the actor fills just a small percentage of the available proscenium space; say 1%. In film, however, every actor (and his face) can become a veritable giant in close-up, a King Kong of character, when his head fills the whole theater proscenium. Talk about the importance of a film actor's movement ... when miniscule autonomic movements of eyelashes, pupils, tips of fingers, edges of the mouth can transfer in magnified proportion the essence of character to a whole audience, and where one slip by the actor is judged by the whole audience.

Movement requirements between theater and film are a trade-off. Once again, it is not the size of the canvas, but the brilliance of the many, many strokes, that determines the great artist on canvas, on stage or on screen. Movement is movement, whatever the size. Great large murals and great small canvases require great artist's technique.

Q: "*Theater actors need to 'turn out' all the time; be more bodily/facially visible to the audience. Doesn't that place a higher burden on a theater act-or?*"

A: No; it creates a trap. Inadequate theater actors (sometimes sadly encouraged by inadequate theater teachers and directors) are forever "turning out," standing on stage with feet askew, like a duck. I know the performer's intent is to be seen full-front as often as possible by the audience, but when I see that particular physicalization all too often exhibited all too often egregiously, I want to shout: "Not even the greatest theater star is watched all the time! Don't overdo the turning out!"

My suggestion for bad actors is to go to the theater and watch how much the audience shifts its attention from one actor to another. Nobody watches any one actor all the time ... no matter how much he is turning out!

A corollary lesson can be drawn from film/video: How often have you attended a movie and watched as the editor shifted the audience's focus of attention from one character to another by "cutting"? The leading character is not on-screen all the time. Sometimes the image on screen focuses on the person listening, not the person talking, and the audience is not disconcerted at all.

Stage actors should learn from that to be selective in their turning-out. Save it for meaningful times, when the audience most needs and wants to focus on your character.

Q: *"The need for truth is heightened in film, whereas in theater it can be avoided."*

A: Truth is truth, so when Auntie and Uncle go to the theater, they deserve the truth as much as their fully-sighted and hearing friends deserve truth in the movie house. The kinesthetic experience—based on a need for emotional truth—is an absolute and democratic necessity in all acting.

Q: *"Film casting directors accuse young theater trained actors of being too theatrical in their film auditions. Does this imply a fundamental difference?"*

A: No. Ten percent of the time this appellation/criticism called "too theatrical" occurs because the good theater actor has forgotten—and needs to be constantly reminded of—the Auntie and Uncle factor when moving from stage to TV and film (where Auntie and Uncle have all those microphones and zoom-lenses and close-ups to help them). Ninety percent of the time, however, and unfortunately, the accusation "too theatrical" means simply bad acting, the result of many theater-trained actors having picked up some bad (false) acting habits in in-adequate theater.

Most young theater actors—and their audiences for that matter—may have seen the greatest film acting—movie house re-runs on TV are everywhere—but they probably have not seen the greatest theater acting. Therefore, under-exposed theater audiences exhibit a higher tolerance for bad acting (unreal "presentational" acting).

This overall lack of exposure to the great theater acting often leads to the development of bad acting habits in such under-exposed young actors, so when they later appear to audition before film casting directors, that bad acting background is called "overly-theatrical" acting ... when it should be properly called "poorly-trained" acting.

Other Witnessing Film Requirements

In film acting, tape "marks"—noting where the actor should stand in performance—are often placed on the set floor to aid in the actor's visual witnessing requirements. The camera operator sets his focus calibrated for those set distances from camera to actor. If the actor misses standing on the mark, he will be filmed out of focus ... not be witnessed. Moreover, the lighting designer has pre-lit those areas where the actor is standing. Thus, missing the "mark" diminishes the clarity of the final image that is transferred to the audience.

In the same way, to further enhance general film witnessing, film actors are often required to refrain from overlapping dialogue (two actors speaking at once when the camera is focused on only one actor in close-up). It is a requirement demanded by the editor in his desire to have a clean, clear sound track for each actor's close-up on-camera dialogue because it facilitates his eventual sound editing.

Similarly, editors often demand physical constancy in various "takes" of a performance—from "wide shot" to "over the shoulder" to "close-up"—to maximize their editing possibilities during later cutting. The performance demand for physical uniformity from take-to-take is called "matching."

However, once again, in these—as in all other instances—of "audience witnessing" requirements, actors must learn to fulfill these requirements without marring the emotional reality of their performances. They must learn within these often difficult and precise physical constraints to remain spontaneously "real" … or they risk creating a performance that is not worth witnessing.

The Director

The director is the pivotal representative of the audience's "witnessing" desires, the audience's conduit to the actor's performance. The director guides the audience's attention to what he thinks is important for the audience to see on stage or on set, and what he believes is crucial for them to hear. In film and video, the good director often asks himself (as the audience's representative): "From what eye and ear position would the *audience* like to experience this scene?" He then adjusts the blocking, camera, voice projection or microphone placements accordingly.

The subsequent editing of the rhythm and succession of the images on screen in film can also be seen as fulfilling this "directorial-guiding" requirement. The director (and his editor) place the film audience—therefore the actor(s) filmed efforts—in an ever-changing and kinesthetic continuum of space and time in order to maximize actor effect on the witnessing audience.

One day I had a new student in class who had just finished a "camera technique" class at another studio. The student, glowing with newly-found knowledge of his learned audience-witnessing capabilities, asked me where I was going to set up the camera in order to film his first class scene with me. He said he had discovered in his camera technique class that his left side was his best side, and the audience would get the best view of his performance from that side. Accordingly, during rehearsal he fussed and fretted about my camera placement—and correspondingly had little concern with emotional technique, feeling, or substance.

Finally, during the shooting, he asked me again where I wanted him to stand vis-à-vis the camera. I told him I wanted him to face away, with his back to camera. He was shocked. He said no one would see him. I said, "With the unemotional performance you've been giving, I think I'm doing you—and the audience—a favor."

Shakespeare said it best: sometimes you have to be cruel to be kind. For the next class, he worked a lot harder on the emotional essence of the scene and less on camera angles.

The lesson of that day—and any day—is this: the actor, however beautifully guided in the witnessing factor by a discerning director, loses all the benefits of that direction if the focus of all that audience-witnessing reveals a false, fake, or inadequate performance.

Another way to look at it: put a lively, real scene behind a dirty, dusty window and the whole neighborhood will have their noses pressed against the glass, but put a dead, purely mechanical scene behind a crystal-clear picture window and few will bother watching.

Surviving a Bad Director

When a director or a self-inducing actor pushes the actor's expressive performance (witnessing requirements) beyond the actor's capability for emotional-truth, the actor should consider himself misdirected. If the director asks the actor to leap up from the couch and throw a glass of water against the wall—and the actor is unfortunately unable to summon up the real and extreme emotion that would make him do that—the actor must fight back, refuse to execute that specific action even if it means an honest admission of his own emotional limitations. One of the best definitions of maturity I know is learning to operate successfully within limitations. Good actors obey it. A good director respects that. Good audiences require it.

The Actor's Obligation in Changing the Shape of a Performance

Let's say I am on the set one day, preparing for a close-up. It is a scene about my mourning; my character's son died, and I am attending the burial. As the actor-as-character, I decide I am filled with abject defeat. My head hangs low. Tears flow. The camera rolls; twenty sorrowful seconds later: "Cut." Everyone applauds.

The director approaches me, frowning. "The camera couldn't see your eyes. We'll have to do it again."

I tell him huffily, "Lower the camera."

He says the camera people can't. It is locked into position by the shape of the set. "Lift your head next time," he tells me, "but … give me the same emotion. It was wonderful."

He walks away. I am incredulous. I mutter to myself, "The same emotion…? Doesn't he know that if I change the shape of the action, the form of my activity, I must change the emotion that gives rise to that action/form? Doesn't he know that new form requires new substance?!"

I settle down, pull myself together and tell the director: "Let's go." The camera rolls. I see the coffin in the grave. I am over-whelmed with memories of my son's death and how much he achieved in his short life. However, in this take, I make sure that a feeling of grief mingles now with pride, as well as sadness. With pride and sadness co-mingled, I hold my head up high and tears flow … legitimately and honestly.

From its restricted angle the camera captures the new form and substance of my acting. The director is happy; I am content. New truth has been co-joined properly with new form.

Summary: Part I
The Five Obligatory Elements

Tablet I is complete.

We have now discussed the Five Obligatory Elements of Good Acting: Conflictual, Real, Honest, Interdependent, and Audience Witnessed.

In achieving these five elements in performance, the actor is only beginning. While these five elements are necessary to a successful performance, they are not sufficient. They can only take the kinesthetic transference of act-or-to-audience a short distance beyond the audience's "willing suspension of disbelief" … but not very far beyond. Once you have mastered the first five elements in your performance, you can call yourself an actor … a beginning actor.

*We must now learn how to be **exciting**; Tablet I implies Tablet II: the Five Enhancing Elements of any acting performance.*

The first three of the five Enhancing Elements (Intensity, Variety, and Complexity) prepare the actor to enter a scene with the richest emotional possibilities.

The final two of the Enhancing Elements (Structure and Elegance) remind the actor that enhanced form increases the explosive power of the resultant actions.

Part II

The Five Enhancing Elements of Good Acting

There Is No **Exciting** *Acting Without Them.*

Intensity
Variety
Complexity
Structure
Elegance

Prologue: Enhancing Elements
"I believe it" versus "There's nothing at risk"

The casting directors, the "guardians at the gate," those human keys at the door of a professional actor's life, often initially assess an actor's audition with a quiet nod, a thank you, and the following phrase: "I believed it." By that they mean they feel the actor's performance was real. They have seen that the actor understands the basic elements of acting (Elements One through Five). She can keep the union card. She is an actor. She has not embarrassed an agent. The agent will not get a negative call from the casting director: "Why the hell did you submit that actor to me? She didn't even understand the first (and second through fifth) thing about acting!"

Unfortunately—and more than sometimes—the next thing out of the casting director's mouth is: "I believed it, but …" (The auditioning actor dies at moments like this) "…there was nothing at stake," which invariably means the performance was not exciting (and it often means goodbye). On the other hand, if they say, smiling "Wonderful; there was a lot at stake in that performance," that means the performance was exciting enough (it included all Elements One through Ten) to get a call back to perform/audition in front of the producers and director.

The acting phrase "at stake" comes from poker playing; in the old mining days, poker players literally put their ownership of a mine claim, or "stake," into the pot in order to have cards dealt to them. Playing "high stakes" poker meant the players could lose their gold mine if they lost the hand, so when someone refers to there being a lot at stake in an actor's performance, it generally means the actor-as-character is performing with such overwhelming depth, breadth, and width of emotional reality that the actor is highly emotionally at risk (being emotionally "at risk" is another favorite auditioner criterion/phrase).

To be at risk, or to "take a risk," or to have a lot at stake while acting on stage is to act with such great excitement, such highly emotional vulnerability and exposure, that the actor is performing at a level of human involvement that the audience is profoundly moved to be in her presence.

At those enhanced performance moments, the actor can be assured of making a much greater impression on the auditioner. Unfortunately, there are the other times when the casting director says there was "nothing at stake" or "there was not enough risk" in an audition. You can generally be assured the next thing they will say is "That was very nice. Thank you. Goodbye. Don't call us; we'll call you."

"At stake" and "at risk" actors climb mountains, not hills. They enter million-dollar poker games, not penny-ante ones. When they traverse tightropes, they do so three thousand feet in the air. Every dealt card, every foothold, is fraught with significance. Every bet, every step toward their goal, is consequential. Actors who create performances emotionally at stake, with much emotionally at risk, are inherently interesting to watch; exciting.

I often tell my students to go to a party during the week and choose the most exciting person they come across, then come to the class next week and describe the person. Without exception, the student initially portrays the person in terms of the first five obligatory elements of good acting: the exciting person is purposeful, goal oriented, and open-minded—without pre-judgment in conversation—honest in their pursuit of a goal; they are people who listen to other people, who allow themselves to have real feelings based on that input; and are comfortable sharing—communicating—their feelings in public. The students generally add that the exciting person invariably is intense, with a wide variety of interests, fascinatingly complex, extremely well-put together—that is, structured—and very smooth and elegant in their actions ... a listing of all the final Enhancing Elements in good acting

An exciting person, on stage or off, is invariably someone who lives and operates according to all Ten Elements of Exciting Life.

"If the actor-as-character's performance isn't important to the actor-as-character, why should it be so to the audience? Personal importance creates intensity."

Chapter 6
Making Sure the Performance is Intense

Only aficionados go to exhibition matches, whereas championship matches attract multitudes. Championship matches involve sudden-death moments—critical moments when the aspects of "do-or-die-there's-no-tomorrow" occur—making these matches quintessentially exciting to watch.

Earlier I offered the words "negotiation'" and "discussion" as gentler synonyms for conflict. By gentler, I mean only in style, never in substance.

An actor-as-character may be whispering, but she is always whispering about something important (at least to her). A woman may be moving across a three-foot high tightrope, but she's emotionally moving across the rope as if her feet were poised 3000 feet over the Grand Canyon. A man may be chasing a butterfly, but the butterfly has deep emotional meaning—import—to that man.

> *Emotional intensity in a performance increases in direct proportion to the actor-as-character's sense of the personal importance of an impending scripted event.*

Importance distills life; it edits experience, which removes the inconsequential. Such condensation creates heat, heat creates light, and the light of an actor's condensed performance draws the audience out of their darkened homes and into the theaters, or melds them into the images on their TV screens.

In our everyday existences, most of us live relatively uneventful, mundane lives, especially when measured against the overall scheme of things. (Human life is a fraction of a fraction of a second on the timeline of the history.) Yet we still cry; we scream; we despair: "I will die if my girlfriend doesn't call me;" "I can't live on $40,000 a year;" "Why does my mother hate me?" all utterances filled with deep and desperate fervor.

When we say such things, we literally mean their gloomy prognostications—although in fact, their statements may arise from nothing more earth-shaking than a cry of despair about losing a girl we've been dating for one month—who has not called us for four days; or the fact we just lost a job we haven't even applied for; or the fact that our mother won't buy us a new prom dress.

These emotional outbursts are often seen as silly, mock operatic to outsiders—nonetheless, they are serious and life-affecting to those of us involved. Strangers—even friends—often refer to these statements as "overly dramatic," characterizing (derisively) people who issue such statements as "actors." "You ought to be an actor," they say, curling a lip, hiding a smile, perhaps raising an eyebrow with faint condescension.

Regardless of their mocking intent, they are literally right. Actors are people who have learned to take everything on stage and on set seriously. Everything in a scene is important to an exciting actor. Even the off-handed joke has a serious intent and belies a purposeful side: it seeks to disarm. The self-deprecating joke's goal is the reduction of self-tension that threatens to immobilize one from important action.

Woody Allen always jokes about sex and death, but they are his neurotic preoccupations in life. He probably thinks about them every day and visits the psychiatrist almost as often to talk about them. It's better to joke about them and reduce some of their emotional weight and pressure before they destroy him, rendering him immobile, unable to take action, on screen and off.

Good actors shun trivialization. Even when actors perform in the classical style of understatement, the understated emotion is never insignificant. Understatement is the cool delivery of a hot substance.

Actors may "throw away" a line, dismiss the seriousness of the moment with an off-handed vocal delivery, but the essential idea remains significant.

A good actor learns to throw away thousand dollar bills, never singles. Understatement is a tactical choice, a stylistic disarming of an opponent through an attempt at creating the illusion of emotional insignificance.

A good technique in making a scene important to an actor—and therefore performed in a more exciting manner—is the following:

Let's say I am hired to play the role of best friend, an adviser in a 2 AM coffee shop scene. Most actors consider that a thankless, non-dramatic role because the scripted dialogue is always about the other character's problems: his angry wife, his job, and his parents; how he wants to break up his marriage, change his job, and punish his parents. My problem as an actor is how do I as the character—the best friend who seems to be simply listening to his problems and focusing on them—make my adviser role important and exciting?

I propose the following actor-as-character self-discussion in rehearsal:

"2 AM?!! Here I am, drinking lousy-tasting, greasy-spoon coffee, talking to this guy about his problems with his job, his wife, and his parents?! I'm losing sleep! More importantly, if my friend doesn't heed my advice to stay with his wife, his job, and his parents ... and is successful and happy doing it ... maybe I was wrong in my life choices: staying married, working at the same job for twenty years, calling my parents every other day. Perhaps I should have married the girl I didn't marry, followed the exciting career I chose not to follow, ignored my parents! Why am I here to advise him?! Like hell I am going to admit I have been wrong all my life! No. My friend is going to follow my advice. He's going to adopt my value system. He's going to stay with his wife, keep his job, and start phoning his parents twice a week, just like I did. What am I, the only fool in town?"

Suddenly, the scene is important to me because the scene has become personal. I am much more ready to play the scene excitingly. The foregoing is a rehearsal/ preparation technique called an *inner-* or *interior-monologue*, through which the actor expresses in her own words during the rehearsal a rendition of the dialogue as it is emotionally important to the actor-as-character.

Michael Shurtleff, in his book *Audition*, also advises the actor seeking importance in a scene to ask himself concerning his character's objective, "What are you fighting for?" thereby imbuing the character's goal with criticalness. If a character is fighting for something, the goal must be significant, thereby creating a performance ten times more likely to be intense and exciting than one where the character is "just" trying to win.

Beware the Word "Just"

The word "just," when defining a character's scene objective, such as "I'm just trying to get my friend to take my advice," "I'm just trying to get a date," or "I'm just looking for a job," diminishes the importance of the character's quest. It reduces the character's objective to the level of unimportance. It creates non-involvement.

The word "just" should be banned at all costs from the actor's lexicon. Nothing the actor does in acting should be "just." "Merely" is another word that should be avoided; it is a cousin to "just."

If an actor is merely creating a performance, just invite me out.

Good actors-as-characters, like good athletes or successful businesspersons, should be irrepressible competitors. Put Michael Jordan or Kobe Bryant on any basketball court and they compete with a fury. It is also said, by the way, that Jordan competes with an equally and unrelenting fury in golf, at a gaming table, or trash-talking. No contest is unimportant for performers like Jordan and Bryant, no venue too small. Their schoolyard games are played as furiously as the NBA playoffs. Little wonder they are two of the most well-known and respected performers/athletes in the world.

Actors could do worse than emulate the passionate involvement of a Michael Jordan or a Kobe Bryant, or for that matter, a tenacious Lance Armstrong, who beat cancer and the long odds of multiple Tour de France victories.

....or Self-Centeredness

Actors are often known, and sometimes criticized, for their strong egos, their concentration on self, the self-importance of their everyday goals. However, such a sense of self-importance may not necessarily be a personality aberration: it may be an occupational necessity.

Good acting requires the development of strong-willed-ness, the commitment to survive and succeed. Survival and success, whether in a scene or in the offstage competition for acting roles, demand the actor to develop and maintain a strong self-aggrandizing point of view. The essential actor's central attitude must be: "If I am to be involved in any scene, it will be important *a priori* no matter the size of my part, its length, or subject matter."

"My character's objective is always important."

It is often said that "There are no small parts; only small actors." Perhaps that is why great actors are so fascinating and compelling to watch. Theirs is an almost automatic acceptance of the importance in any enacted event in which they participate, no matter how small the role. That heightened attitude increases the actor's human systemic involvement in any scene, resulting in the fullness of the actor's expressive components. Blood flows more readily to their mind, muscles, and voice box. Their hearing is more acute, their eyes sparkle with focus.

Notice that good and successful actors rarely blink; their eyes always seem open and luminescent. It occurs because they are so intensely focused on the scene in the world around them. Cutting off visual information from an actor's external reality, even due to the briefest blink, even for an instant, is so antithetical to the need for information-gathering that their eyes can only afford to rest, to blink, a minimal amount, and only then at the least critical times in the scene. The more important the task, the more it unconsciously necessitates an actor-as-character to commit all their sensory resources to winning.

That recognition of scene-importance, and the resultant heightened stimulation, causes actors-as-characters to dig deeper into their personal emotional capital to win. Heart, soul, feeling, and mind are maximally-engaged in the task at the fullest levels. Life takes on a pressured reality. What was mildly interesting before becomes subsequently exciting … almost dangerous.

Listen in everyday life to the timbre and weight of the human voice when someone is talking about something important (for them). Their vocal volume does not necessarily increase, nor do pace or pitch, but due to maximum cellular involvement in manufacturing the vocal tone—all the synapses are connected at important moments—there is a weight, a resonance in the voice that causes strangers to turn, to recognize that something important is being discussed.

Think of the times you were sitting in a restaurant and oblivious to the many chattering conversations around you, when suddenly one conversation caught your attention. You turned; you listened. You looked at the conversationalists. Their faces, their eyes, the tilt of their bodies all reflected the importance of their talk. If you had asked the conversationalist what they were talking about, I'll bet they would have said that they were talking about something "important" to them.

Sports use the term "sudden death" to describe an overtime game; it is revealing and instructive. Good actors should try as much as is logical to take the conflict between them and their opponents to life-threatening proportions (at least psychologically and emotionally). A good actor always stands at the edge of a high precipice; a better actor stands with his toes over the edge; the best actors have half of each foot over the edge … and a strong wind blowing at their back!

Let's say I am a producer. I am going to offer you a role, a mountain climber, in my next film. You will be on screen two minutes. I am busy, so I want you to design your own scene.

You more likely than not will decide in the following manner: "My character's mother will be in the hospital, needing an expensive, life-saving cancer operation. The mountain summit I am to climb will be humongously high and located in Tibet. A million dollars in gold will be at the top of the climb. The face of the mountain will be severe and rocky. Night will be falling. A thousand foot fall will occur at any misstep. My left foot will be frost-bitten. My hands will be bleeding. The blizzard will be raging…."

"All right," the actor says, "I get your point. A good actor would want everything in a scene to be important, and I theoretically agree with you—importance increases a performance's intensity and excitement—but how many actors are offered scenes about climbing mountains in blizzards, much less find a producer who will let them design their own scene? Lately, I have been given dull scenes to perform; scenes that are unimportant, fundamentally insignificant. For example: my character's goal is to catch a butterfly. Or … go out on a date with a nerdy boy. Or … play a woman buying a ten dollar wristwatch in a drugstore. How can I attach major importance to scenes like that?"

I answer: "Do you attach supreme importance to everyday events of your own personal life? How many times have you've cried and complained about a developing bald spot, a traffic ticket, or the new girl of your dreams becoming the old girl of your nightmare? Well, if you can attach deep emotional importance to these seemingly inconsequential events in your everyday life, why can't you do the same in a character's life?"

I suggest that actors implement Uta Hagen's suggestion on substitution: "Take a substituted psychological reality [from the actor's own life] and transfer it to the existing circumstances and events in the play: transfer the essence of the experience to [the facts of] the scene. Make every character you perform personally important … the same as you do in your everyday life." If your everyday life can be emotionally important to you, so can—and should—it be for any character you play in a scene.

Through the Particular, the Universal

Isn't there a corollary risk in making a scene too personal? Won't the performance perhaps become so specifically unique to me—the actor-as-character—that it loses its universal relevance to the audience?

The answer to that possible conundrum is best conceptualized by the Greek philosopher, Aristotle, over 2,000 years ago: "Through the particular, we find the universal." Incidentally, that notion not only became the concept central to his whole philosophical stance, but it also turned out to be the basis for much of Western civilization's subsequent scientific inquiry.

When an acting scene has profound personal relevance to the particular actor, when the emotional chords that are struck in the actor-as-character in the scene go so deep, deeper than the topical truths of the scene—when the personal resonance emanates from beyond sociological implications, beyond even the psychological truths—when the character's truth moves deeper than gender and age to a philosophical level, to a common humanity, if you will, a humanity that encapsulates a shared emotional fundamentalism in all people (reason versus passion; right versus wrong; good versus bad); at that point, the exciting actor lives at a level of common universal human truth, one that underlies the particular facts in the scene ... and finds emotional traits shared by all humanity.

At the deepest level of an actor's emotional involvement in portraying a character, that performance is no longer simply about a character who is a particularly poor person, a particularly co-dependent poor person, a particularly young female co-dependent poor person; it is about the universal struggle, the universal emotional experience underlying all struggles of poor and rich, young and old, male and female, independent and co-dependent; it reverberates with universal truth. When operating at such a deep level of emotional fact, the fundamental nature of all humanity is experienced by the actor-as-character in her particular performance; it resonates with universal philosophical human implications deeper than all particulars ... and touches the audience deeply, and intensely—and universally.

"Steak for appetizer, steak for main course, steak for a side dish, steak for dessert, and steak juice for aperitif and after-dinner drink, no matter how brilliantly tasty the steak may be, is boring. Variety is the spice of life."

Chapter 7
Making Sure the Performance is Varied

An Olympic decathlon champion is considered the world's greatest athlete, in spite of the fact that often he has probably never been a record holder or world champion in any single event! Instead, the Olympic decathlete's superiority is based on wide-ranging excellence in performing ten varied events over a brief two-day period: the discus throw, the high hurdles, the 100-meter dash, the high jump, the pole vault, the 200-meter dash, the javelin throw, the 400-meter run, the shot put and the mile run. The decathlon is the consummate test of the range—horizontal excellence—of an athlete's ability.

The same holds for actors: An exciting actor is an emotional decathlete capable of feeling many varied emotions in a short scene/time. He is one who is able to feel and exhibit within the scene the widest range of emotional experience both possible and logical to the character being performed.

Watching a good actor perform with Olympic variety in a scene is like being guided through a ten-room mansion. Each internal room has a different size and shape; each internal room is accented in a different color; each room serves different functions.

The audience member moves through that unified yet multi-varied performance house as if he is moving through the wide range of a person's (character's) entire life, ageless and timeless, experiencing many different styles, colors, and "feels" within it.

Audiences are rational consumers of emotional experience, prudent-buyers of feeling who want their money's worth in watching and experiencing a performance. When audience members enter a theater to witness a performance, they expect a ten-course meal of emotions, a variety of emotional experience in their kinesthetic involvement with the actors, to facilitate a broader, more exciting contact with itself. They want their own fully "discovered self" for their money! To wit, when an audience leaves a memorable performance, what they are really remembering is their own emotional experience in the presence of that performer.

To satisfy a variety-hungry audience, a director can hire many different actors in one scene, each serving up their own specialized (emotional) dish to the audience; that is, one particular actor in the scene to do an angry character, one particular actor to do a sad character, one particular actor to do a sexy character. Isn't that what "character-actors" are: specialists in one emotional "type"? Or the director can hire just one actor to serve up a full course meal himself, seven emotional courses in a single scene. Isn't that what leading actors are? They lead us with the breadth of their emotional comprehensiveness to the deepest total enjoyment of ourselves. Perhaps that's why leading actors are paid so much: they do such a variety of emotional jobs in any one scene.

The Rule of Seven

When approaching a role in a scene, I encourage the good actor to look for the widest array of emotional possibilities in the scene and/or character, thereby enabling them to turn their single performance into a star-turn, a ten-event decathlon, a meal of multi-dished emotional possibilities.

If any actor wants in his career to play increasingly larger and better roles—to extend the range of his career beyond small parts, to create highly visible performances of such emotional variety that creates wide-ranging audience excitement—the actor must train and practice as an emotion-decathlete. He must train to overcome all emotional narrowness, to counter emotional atrophy, to forgo any hesitancy to feel, and be able in his career to use the whole spectrum of his personal emotional possibilities.

To put into practice this capability for emotional variety, I suggest the actor should look for at least seven different emotional tactics/possibilities in any scene or performance.

Seven? Why not ten, twenty, fifty?

Granted, seven is an arbitrary number; however, seven choices pose a respectable challenge for the actor, yet, at the same time, not so much of a challenge that it is off-putting. Ten is too formidable; three is too easy. Seven has a "golden mean" ring about it; it enables an actor to expand his emotional horizons, but not so much so that the actor goes numb. The quest for variety shouldn't put an actor into protective emotional shock: how much feeling can an actor take at once?

All right; you don't like seven? Choose eight; nine; ten ... fifty. I don't care ... as long as the challenging emotional performance stretch is attempted by you and you don't run out of time and get emotionally spent. Like all other all rehearsal techniques, the aim here is to rehearse the actor for future possibilities, not to create any set of arbitrary fixed finalities.

The dissenting actor argues: "What if the scene has only one or two emotions at best? Let's say I am playing an 'angry-young-man,' and I have three dialogue pages with nothing but curses and epithets? Aren't the possibilities for variety somewhat circumscribed in a scene like that?"

No; not if you are a good actor-decathlete. Variety is always possible. Think of it this way: if the scene performance is supposed to last three pages, that's a long time on stage or screen. A good actor must create variety no matter how emotionally repetitive the scene (curses and all) seems ... I repeat, seems ... at first glance. Once again: audiences are prudent buyers who want a wide range of kinesthetic involvement, especially at Broadway prices of $100 a ticket!

They want variety!

By the way, who says an angry, epithet-tossing young man has to be exclusively or mono-dimensionally angry anyway? Couldn't his anger be co-mingled with humor, confusion, bemusement, and sadness? For example: "I'm angry in the scene because you shocked me; I'm angry here because you made me sad; I'm angry here because you made me jealous; I'm angry in this section because you make the whole thing seem uproariously and ironically funny." Each moment has anger at the core, but multiple shades of it.

Another example: I go to an art gallery to buy a red painting, I don't expect the seller to show me an exclusively red painting, a monochromatically red canvas! When I say I want red, I want mainly red, principally red, predominantly red, but not exclusively red. I want perhaps a red painting that includes some pinks and yellows blended in, and perhaps even a hint of black to serve as stark contrast to the overall exciting red. Even Picasso, when he painted his *Blue Boy*, used multiple shades of blue.

The good actor, when attempting to discover variety in a seemingly monochromatic scene, should rehearse the whole scene multiple times, each time according to differing emotional possibilities: once entirely angrily, once entirely sadly, once entirely happily. In that way, he is forced to find a range of truth and reality possibilities in any single scene, and when he subsequently gives a final performance, he will have discovered and can perform a series of moments with a wide variety of emotional possibilities. Scenes, life, drama, dialogue are almost infinitely elastic in terms of emotional meaning.

A dear professor friend many years ago was an expert witness for the defense in the Henry Miller obscenity trial. As he was seated in the witness chair, the cross-examining prosecutor asked my friend if he ever used such vile, offensive, and depraved language as Miller used in his books *Tropic of Cancer* and *Tropic of Capricorn* (the lawyer quoted the most obscene passages). He paused, waiting for my friend's answer.

My friend paused in return, looked at his wife, who had accompanied him to the trial that day, demurely seated in a nearby row, paused again, and then finally answered, "Only when making love to my wife."

She smiled sweetly; dare I say innocently? The defense rested.

By rehearsing any scene multiple times, with varied emotional attacks, the actor can soon discover the widest—and often unexpected—range of emotional possibilities inherent in any scene.

The Rule of Seven: Line by Line

To move the actor even farther away from any tendency to choose one emotional tack for an entire scene, I suggest that the Rule of Seven can be applied to each line in a scene. Yes; I am suggesting there can be (and at least) seven possible different emotional motivations for any one line.

The usual skeptical actor retorts: "What about the instance where the writer, above the line 'I hate you,' adds the parenthetical notation '(in anger).' That seems pretty cut and dried! The writer wants to the actor to feel anger. What other emotional choice does the actor have?"

Writers are not infallible. While often brilliant, they are not gods; at least most of the writers I know. Therefore, their parenthetical instructions in a script should be seen as suggestions, not commandments. Granted, suggestions from experts (after all, the writer, having written the script, has lived with the character longer than the actor has—at least initially), but writer's directions should be viewed only as suggestions from one expert to another.

Out of respect, when the actor goes through the scene the first time, he should enact the character emotionally as the writer suggests; in the above case: angrily. But, after one or two initial interpretive rehearsal passes, it becomes the actor's turn to live with the character. Just as a father and mother must pass the son or daughter along to other parents to have grandchildren, so must a writer pass on the script to actors to create final living performances out of it.

If the writer (and many writers are on set producers and/or directors) balks at any of the actor's subsequent emotional attempts to interpret the line and demands again the emotion be played as the script indicates, I suggest that the actor—as a professional—play the character as the writer suggests ("the man who pays the piper calls the tune"). When the shoot is over, I would also suggest—pointedly but nicely—that the actor ask the writer to re-read the texts of Shakespeare, Moliere, Ibsen, Arthur Miller, and Tennessee Williams, great playwrights all. Each used few, if any, definitive stage directions—emotional suggestions—in their scripts, yet they seem to get some great varied performances of their plays by a wide range of script-interpretive actors.

Back to the skeptical actor's question: "How many different emotional ways can you possibly say, 'I hate you?'" Well, let's initially bow to the writer's suggestion, anger, which is emotion number one: "I hate you" … said with red-faced venom. Number two: what about sadness? There is nothing sadder than hating someone you once loved. "I hate you," he says, tears to follow. How about surprise … to suddenly discover you hate someone when a moment before you had thought you loved them? Or calmness? "I hate you," he says, coldly, factually, without regret. ("Revenge is a meal best served cold," they say.) How about sexiness: "I hate you," because you turn me on … even now … and even though—perhaps, *especially* now—that I hate you. (Did you ever make love to somebody after a knock-down, drag-out fight? Possible, yes? Sometimes even cathartically pleasurable?) Another possibility is amusement: "I hate you," but I must admit you make me laugh. We have such a silly relationship. Or confusion: "I hate you" … yet, at the same time, I love you … and want you … it's all very confusing. A final choice: exhausting; "I hate you," you make me feel very bone-wearingly tired because we're stuck in this relationship with no exit.

The skeptical actor concedes: "All right, then. Emotional variety is possible in any single scene or line of dialogue, but what criteria do you use for choosing the best among all these alternatives? Some menus have too many choices, don't they?

Yes, therefore I suggest the following choice criteria:

1. All emotional choices must always be true to human behavior (logical; in order to be real)!

2. Look for the most unexpected emotion for the actor-as-character to feel at a particular time in performance.

3. Look for one that offers the most complexity in the character.

4. Make the choice extend the range of character feelings in the scene (or whole play or film), one that takes the actor and audience into unique areas of emotion, into feelings the character has not or will not have felt before in any other portions of the scene.

Once again, variety is the spice of life.

Personal Courage and Variety

Emotions being tactics, when conflictual life is engaged in by emotionally open, courageous, and goal-oriented actors, variety in performance is automatically present. Variety is the tactical logic of courageous competitors. When emotional tactic #1 fails, the smart and courageous and win-oriented actor-as-character automatically moves to emotional choices #2, #3, #4, as required.

"Here's my sadness, now give me what I want." "Here's my anger, now give me what I want." "My sexiness..."

Winners never stay with losing tactics too long. An actor who plays a whole scene fixated on a single emotion is generally a frightened actor. They have found—and wish to remain in—their emotional comfort zone rather than try to stretch their emotional resources in a courageous attempt to win. "You, actor-as-character, seem to be more committed to being angry … or sad, or confused, or frightened … than actually changing your situation by winning."

Imagine a football game where the halfback keeps running "off-tackle," charging at the same spot in the defense throughout the entire game, over and over again, in spite of being tackled for a loss on every play! The coach would shout at that player: "Are you more interested in running off tackle or winning? Try an end-run, pass the ball, find a tactic that works! What are you afraid of?"

My "rule of seven" is an active rehearsal attempt to force an instinctively timorous actor to consciously explore—perhaps beyond the actor's normal comfort zone of emotion—varied emotional strategies within the scene. The intent is for the actor willfully to counteract his own initial deficient instinct, which is, after all, what all acting training, techniques, and exercises are designed to do: apply conscious will when unconscious instinct is deficient.

The "Cookie Girl"

How does a person get fixated on one or two emotions in their everyday operative reality? What keeps humans—actors—from being emotionally/courageously flexible—varied—in the pursuit of our goals?

An illustrative story: "When I was a little girl, Mama used to make cookies in our kitchen. One day, I went into the kitchen and said assertively, 'Mama, I want a cookie.'

"Mama looked at me. 'Don't talk to me in that tone of voice.' Head hanging, I exited the kitchen and put away my assertiveness; it got me no cookies.

"Two hours later, Daddy came home. I greeted him at the door. 'Daddy, I want a cookie.'

'Don't whine,' he said. 'My secretary whines all day.'

"No cookies there, either. Put whining in the same closet as assertiveness!

"But I still wanted a cookie, so a half hour later, I skipped into the kitchen where Mommy and Daddy were cooking, made a funny face, and said cutely, 'Laura wants a coo-kieee.' They laughed, scooped me up in their arms, and gave me two cookies. I became a cookie-girl, eternally cute, always operating with a sing-song voice."

Fast forward.

"I am now thirty-five years old. I am still a bright, cute, easy-to-scoop-up-in-your-arms cookie girl. I have surrounded myself with people—including a husband and children—who accede to the wishes of (that is, gives cookies to) people who are funny-faced and say things in a cute-voice. Constant success reinforces my lifelong pattern.

"Then, my husband dies. I am independent. I need a job. Everyone tells me how cute I am. I decide to become an actress, so I join an acting class.

"I tell the teacher I like to do cute roles, but my acting teacher says no, I'm too old. She says my face and body have progressed beyond cuteness. She wants me to do assertive roles, perhaps even whiny roles, but I tell her I don't know how to do that anymore. My assertive and whiny muscles have long since atrophied from lack of use.

"So, like many other actors, I go to another teacher, who also wants me to expand my role-playing repertoire in the same direction as well. I leave her.

"During all this, I get an agent; I press him to find me a job. My agent tells me in a post-feminist world all the best roles are for strong women: lawyers, doctors, business owners. Even a whiny wife would be better than a just-cute non-entity. We fight; my agent drops me.

"I am out of the acting business; I'm applying for a job as a cute greeter at Wal-Mart."

Don't be Over-Insured

Emotional inflexibility is like tidal insurance. If you grow up on the coast of Hawaii and every few years a tidal wave destroys your house, you soon learn to buy tidal insurance. Twenty years later, you're living in Nebraska and you're still carrying the tidal insurance policy. A friend asks you, "Why are you still paying for tidal insurance?" You say, "I remember when I was a kid…."

Paying for outdated emotional tidal insurance is like protecting against future negative possibilities that no longer can possibly happen: it is a waste of resources. Smart actors must revisit their emotional insurance plans from time to time to consider canceling, or at least lessening, their coverage.

First Choices

Actors: beware your first choices in analyzing a scene and character. Human mental and emotional systems are inherently defensive in nature; they have evolved to protect us, to temper life's vicissitudes, to reduce the shocks and blows that random experience is capable of raining down on us. Most actors (even the good ones) when confronted by a new reality—such as looking at a new script—almost always initially apply their defensive systems: they naturally and logically compute the average concept first, the median possibility, the predictable safe choice. (These safe choices are perhaps best for everyday life, but they are almost always antithetical to exciting acting life.)

One day I was working with an exceptionally talented and usually emotionally brave actor to prepare him for a role. We were having difficulty interpreting one section of one scene. No matter how many times I tried to encourage him to pursue the emotional arena I was suggesting. I failed. He completely resisted my entreaties.

We went to lunch. As we were walking to the dining room to join his wife, he said to me: "I hate the scene. It's a poorly written piece of …. I'm going to call the writer to re-write it." He was adamant, furious, frustrated.

This generally rambunctious attitude carried over into a slight disagreement with his wife at lunch, during which he acted toward her exactly as I had suggested he act in the scene. I said nothing, but I mentally recorded the event.

After lunch we went back to work. When he picked up the phone to call the writer, I said, "Before you do, consider this: the emotional performance you gave just now with your wife is exactly what I am asking you to consider in the script."

He stared at me. After a long pause, he said, sheepishly, "Did I do that with her? I hate myself when I do that." We thereby discovered why he had avoided the emotional acting choice—even to the point of denial—and did not understand during rehearsal what I was talking about.

No one is immune from paying tidal insurance. Sometimes even what we think is a brave choice often resembles its cowardly twin: learned caution. The human circuits of impulse and fear run very close to one another. They can be thought of as shadow images of one another, often indistinguishable. Such proximity often leads to second-guessing, a particularly pernicious disease.

I encourage in rehearsal even the bravest of actors to visit second, third, fourth … even fifth, sixth and seventh possible choices. Refusal to consider possibilities is a devastating acting illness. We can all—even the bravest of us—be the captives of unconscious fears, prejudgments, or prejudices. Good actors work hard to avoid them.

"Art keeps alive what is yet to be fully known. When life is fully known and capable of being replicated, we give it to science. Actors are artists, not scientists."

Chapter 8
Making Sure the Performance is Complex

Great performances invariably embrace the great unresolved issues of human existence, keeping those universal concerns at the forefront of the audience's consciousness; or, as James Joyce said in his book *Portrait of the Artist as a Young Man*, the artist must "forge in the smithy of my soul the uncreated conscience of my race."

The great actor, therefore, only by putting herself through a complex emotional experience vis-à-vis the conflict—where no singular right or singular wrong exists (the philosopher Hegel said great tragedy is not created by positing right versus wrong, but by positing right versus right)—can activate the fullness and richness of the audience's life.

Great dramatists—and actors—must eagerly pose and explore the often still-irresolvable issues of human existence: Should one "love not wisely but too well?" (Shakespeare). Is it better to "settle for half" [of life's passion] or to safely pursue a muted existence? (Arthur Miller). Is family duty or social duty paramount in the life of a group or society? (Sophocles).

There are no easy answers: both sides have equal seduction and equally valid arguments. I often think the truly complex and revealing tragedy of Adolph Hitler's evil (yet to be written) may lie in his belief that he was doing good for Germany, and the great drama about Mother Theresa would be that she doubted her faith and convictions right until the end of her saintly life.

Many years ago, I had the good fortune to direct the brilliant actor Raul Julia in a film. Before every scene we sat and analyzed long and hard before mutually agreeing on the emotional essence of his character in the scene. Then, always, as he started away toward the set for filming, he'd stop, turn, and we'd say to each other, "And yet...." That was our code for expressing that "the exact opposite might also be true."

Raul entered every scene with a complex set of emotional possibilities.

Contradiction is inherent in all life. Just as with exciting people, exciting characters contain paradox, contradiction, irony, mutual opposition and absurdity. They simultaneously love and hate. They are concurrently brave and cowardly. They are mutually certain and confused.

When stimulus from a scene occurs to a simple actor, it echoes singularly, with monochromatic dullness, as if off the walls of a one room cave. But when it echoes in the stage life of an exciting actor, one who has in rehearsal dug through the cavern walls of her own deepest life, who has deeply explored all sides of all issues, who has through a career of complex emotional rehearsal process become a high-ceilinged, multi-roomed, hollowed-out, expansive grotto of feeling, that stimulus resonates profoundly, over and over again, like the eternal inner voices in the caves of E.M. Forster's *Passage to India*.

On the other hand, an actor who enters a scene without sufficient appreciation of—and preparation for—the depth and resonance of human complication possible in the scene, will find their acting craft flying very low to the ground ... and will generally crash in performance hell, in the unremitting and all-consuming implosion of audience boredom.

A good actor must remember that complexity is the proper and best emotional fuel for a high-flying performance.

Self-Debate

Good acting can be seen as "... a riddle, wrapped in a mystery, inside an enigma ..." (to quote Winston Churchill).

When is the right time to pull the plug on our beloved mother's life support system? When is war justified? Is brutal torture ever justified to discover information that could save thousands of lives? What is the exact definition of "viable" in a fetus or any born child: is a one-year-old crawling alone in an alley "viable"? Which of your children do you save from a burning house if only one can be saved?

There are no universally agreed-upon answers to these questions; only, it seems, continuing questions and proper debate.

The good actor must accept the universal complexity of a deeply-lived life, and if she does so, she will always live as the character in such a perpetual state of inner self-debate.

Drama that neatly decides an issue without any doubt, with the participating actors-as-characters in those dramas resolving these inner and outer conflicts too easily—often before performance —creates political theater.

Political theater tries to settle character questions for the audience, giving them only one side of the issue, the author's, or the director's or the actors'. Such political theater—propaganda, really—is ultimately boring because it offers ready-made, simplistic answers to complex issues. It becomes children's theater in the most pejorative sense: "Don't think for yourself; just do as Mommy—in this case, the writer or actor—says."

Political theater is preaching to the choir … which may enthrall the members of the choir, but generally bores the rest of the congregation/audience, who seek to be moved beyond prejudice to a deeper truth.

Polemic art is dishonest art because it prejudges the outcome, fixes the game. Its purpose is not art—not even education; its purpose is propaganda—pure politics.

Pre-Judgment

Actors, therefore, who enter a scene having prejudged a character, who choose to play an "asshole"-character or an "obscene whore"-character, who by dint of terminology adjudicate in their preparation the right and wrong of their character's personality (thereby deciding in advance the character's relative merits), are acting dishonestly and all too sloppily. They are overlooking their primary acting task: to *advocate* in their performance the complexity and contradiction of their character's position and let the audience decide for themselves the character's personality/fate.

In support of that position advocating complexity in performance, I offer this experience from my everyday life: I've never met an asshole who thought of themselves as an asshole, and most whores I've met rarely think of themselves as whores. (The former would state they are misunderstood, and the latter would state they are simply working girls and boys, women and men.)

Exciting reality demands complex perspectives. Actors who enact their characters with quick judgments invariably present a performance that is predetermined and simplistic, and thereby cheat the audience.

Pre-digesting a character creates pabulum for the masses. Such acting assumes audiences are intellectual babies who need to be spoon-fed. Such actors underestimate the audience; even if the audience is young and inexperienced, they are capable of complex feelings; character offerings to them should be nothing less.

To prepare complex characters, good actors should approach their characters as if the actors were *defense lawyers*, not judges; emotional advocates of their client-actor-as-character's position, not adjudicators.

In preparing for a good performance, a good actor's attitude should be: "Your honor, members of the jury—to wit, my audience—my character (into whose shoes I am stepping) may seem like an asshole or obscene whore to the opposing side, and perhaps even to the rest of the world, but if you look closely, review my performed character's life in detail, you will find a more than defensible human being, a complex human being worthy of achieving sympathy—if not victory—in his objective quest for your empathy."

This approach—character-advocacy—allows the audience, through their kinesthestic response capabilities, to make the assessment of the character(s) complex traits on their own, and allows the audience through that process of sensory kinesthesia to access their own personal complex characteristics. Good actors accept that it is the audience's job and not the actor's to make the final judgments on a performed character's worth—judgements that should occur only after the full performance/trial is over, when all the evidence of the drama or comedy has been played out and kinesthetically experienced.

> *A great play or film is a fair and complex search for truth; as such, it delays judgment until all the facts are known. It is based on everyday life, on the adversary system wherein each character offers their personal defense of their actions. It is the scheme upon which everyday common law is based, one in which both sides are vigorously and fairly argued.*

On the other hand, when the actor-as-character's performance is nothing more than a pre-judged trial, it is a kangaroo court; the resolution of the drama is pre-ordained, creating bad justice, bad acting, and worse, dull theater.

Elements of Acting Complexity

Simultaneity of Feeling

Human emotion is never a discrete occurrence. In everyday life an experienced single emotion does not end and another begins. Emotions overlap. They are like musical notes of a piano, when the pianist plays the musical score with a depressed foot pedal, blending subsequent sounds over time.

The rise and fall of human emotion operates like pistons, all part of a single moving engine: one piston may be dominant at a particular moment, one emotion coming to the highest point of the human engine's actions but, again, like a piston, all emotions in the actor's engine are co-existent and concurrently operative: "I'm mostly angry at this moment, but, at the same time, I'm also sad and feeling sexy … while I'm also at once confused and hurt."

Contradiction

Newton's Second Law of Thermodynamics states that "For each action there is an opposite and equal reaction" occurring simultaneously. Walt Whitman, in his poem *Leaves of Grass*, states it thus: "Do I contradict myself? Oh, well, I contradict myself. I contain multitudes." All life—and therefore all great art—is unavoidably rooted in contradiction. Life is a product of simultaneous oppositional forces: matter and anti-matter, being and nothingness, yin and yang.

As in the twists and turns of everyday life, when a human being turns left, the other part of her continues going straight or to the right.

As confirmation, I suggest an actor attempt the following experiment: go to a safe place and drive a car straight ahead for some time, then make a left turn. Note the following: when you suddenly make the turn to the left, your whole body refuses to make the full turn. Part of your body still maintains forward direction.

Suddenly make a right turn. While part of your body reacts to the momentum of the new right turn, part of you will still be responding to both the earlier forward and left momentum. In point of fact, your body will be going in all three contradictory directions at once. So it is with emotions: one direction dominates while the others coexist.

Thus, contradiction and simultaneous occurrences are built into the very construct of living and, therefore, once again, must be present in a good actor's real performance. (That inner contradiction is sometimes called the character's "inner conflict.")

I had an Asian student once who was very, very shy. At the age of thirty, he had never dated—much less kissed—a woman. His mother was taking him soon to Korea where she had arranged a marriage for him, but before he left, he took his last acting class. I serendipitously gave him a scene where he had to kiss a girl. He frowned, and said adamantly that it was impossible for him to do so, especially in public. I asked him to at least hug her. After considering a long moment, he said he would.

The scene began. The hugging moment arrived. He stared at the actress. His whole body leaned toward her. The dynamic tension in his body—his inner conflict, if you will—was compelling, but he couldn't do the hug. When the scene was over, I asked him what happened.

He said, "My body says 'yes,' my mind says 'no.'" It was the sweetest, most striking and affecting example of inner contradiction I had ever seen.

"Opposites"
Michael Shurtleff, in *Audition*, suggests actors in their performance, as a means of creating complexity, create a condition of "opposites," one of his "Ten Guideposts" to make an actor's performance more interesting and richer in resonance. He suggests that if an actor-as-character loves another actor in the scene, she should also hate them; if she desires someone, she should also be afraid of them.

A warning on the label of this approach, however: improper utilization of the concept of "opposites" can result in bad acting. For example, inadequate, but well-meaning, actors all too often try to play those states of "opposites" or contradiction sequentially. That is, they first enact one emotional side, then the other: first love, then hate; desire, then fear; happiness, then sadness;

one side of a polarity, then the other side. But ... the good actor must remember Newton's Law: those "opposites" must occur simultaneously.

The human linear mind (and therefore the actor's voluntary system in performance) can no more consciously "play" contradiction or opposites than a human being can fully understand a universe where matter and non-matter co-exist, a universe constantly expanding at an accelerated rate to infinity, or time bending back on itself ... or any of the other multitudes of life's paradoxical conundrums. (All right ... perhaps Einstein and Stephen Hawking could ... and a few of their colleagues ... but they are a score of geniuses out of billions.)

Human cognition does not logically embrace paradox, dichotomy, or "opposites" (hence the human need for and capability of poetry, with its all-inclusive metaphors, similes, and images, that are not limited to linear logic). The cognitive, logical mind is sequential, not simultaneous. Feeling, on the other hand, is non-coincident, and cognitive logic is structured mightily to reconcile, not necessarily explain, emotional contradiction.

What Shurtleff recognized in his years of Broadway auditioning and viewing, what he saw operative in great actors—and what his guidepost of "opposites" implicitly encourages actors to manifest in performance—is this: great actors consistently perform at real, deep, and complex levels of emotional reality, and, therefore, automatically live in the desirable and exciting condition of Newtonian opposites.

All good actors should do the same.

Cliff Osmond

If the good actor, seeking complexity in performance, lives in performance deeply, automatically, and unconsciously, the audience-compelling complex conditions of contradiction and opposites—and paradox—will occur.

The Unexpected/Unknown

Audiences often say of their fellow exciting actors, "I love watching them. You never know what they are going to do next." The reason: exciting actors don't quite know what they are going to do next! The Danish philosopher Kierkegaard said, "Logic can take you to the brink, but only a leap of faith can take you beyond."

The good actor in performance recognizes, accepts, and appreciates many of his best "choices" take place *au passant*, in passing, during the performance, activated by his creative unconscious rather than from any consciously defined choices or pre-suppositions made in pre-performance rehearsal.

There is a jazz element in good acting. The script and the director give the actor her melodic line, however variably constricted or free as it may be, and the playing actor improvises within those melodic strictures, bringing to every performance the spontaneous sounds and rhythms of her feelings.

I sometimes ask young actors how much they know of themselves, how much they are aware of the deepest vicissitudes of their emotional lives. The youngest say 85 percent; the middle-aged say 50 percent. I tell them I am down to two percent ... and the amount is declining from there. The experiencing of life, whether onstage or off, is inevitably much fuller and richer than a purely analytical grasp of it.

When an excellent, practiced, and complex actor subsequently sees their performance on the screen, they are often as surprised by their performance—by their own (sub-conscious) acting choices—as the rest of the audience. "Oh, my God ... so that's what I am when I am under that kind of pressure. Amazing?! My love has elements of sadness in it and sexual need. Oh, my God, look at my confusion! I'll be damned."

An actor's surprise/discovery in reviewing her performance is a good sign because it means that the actor had been living at a performance level of such complexity that even the actor herself had no idea what she was emotionally capable of achieving.

Complex Style: "Playing Against"

As a young actor, I was six foot five, with an acne-scarred face, and weighed over three hundred pounds. Accordingly, I was cast mostly as "heavies," the nasty characters.

One day I was on a set with a few fellow heavies in a cowboy TV show, having just finished our final scene rehearsal. We were to threaten a store owner in a Western town.

Between takes we were sitting, relaxed, waiting for our turn to film when the Assistant Director called us. As we approached the set, one of the most experienced actors leaned over to me and said fatherly, "Kid, when you say that line to the store owner, 'I'm going to kill you,' smile. It'll work better."

I respected the actor, so I took his advice to heart. When it came to me to film the scene, and the director said "Action!" I said my line to the store owner, "I'm going to kill you," and instead of glowering with hate as I had done in rehearsal, I smiled.

The director immediately said, "Cut!" He walked over to me. "What the hell were you smiling about? You looked positively goofy."

The fatherly Heavy leaned over and whispered in my ear. "I forgot to tell you, kid: smile on the outside, but on the inside, you still got to hate."

The technique the Heavy was trying to instruct me in is an acting condition called "playing against," which occurs when the textual action—the dialogue or other physical action—operates in dynamic opposition, contradiction, to the sub-textual emotion being felt.

"Playing against," creating a conflict between outer style and inner substance, manifests a complexity of behavior that audiences find intriguing. Witness Hannibal Lector, the serial killer in *Silence of the Lambs*, who continually smiles warmly and speaks quietly—rather than glowering with hate and shouting—as he discusses eating the flesh of his adversary. Probably one of the reasons Anthony Hopkins, who played Lector, is considered one of the greatest actors of his generation is that he always brings to his acting roles such great inner-versus-outer complexity. I recently read that he is considering ceasing his acting career because he doesn't know if he has the energy to dig so deeply—and with such great complexity—into himself for another role.

Great acting is hard, complex work; that's why producers pay lots of money to great actors to do it.

"Substance without shape is like a body without bones: an unsupportable mass destined by gravity to fall on its face."

Chapter 9
Making Sure a Performance is Structured

The Benefits of Structure

Life is structure: periodic tables; $E=MC^2$; gravity; the ebb and flow of the tides of the ocean; the changing of the seasons; the fixed and regulated forms of atoms and molecules. Even in the philosophical explanations of "chaos theory," the search for an intellectual explanation of a seemingly random universe is a structured effort. Intellectualism is the product of the mind, which itself is *sine qua non* structural.

Good acting, therefore, since it must adhere to all of life's emotional reality, must have structure, and enhanced structure in performance benefits the good actor in several ways:

1. It shortens the audience's time-perception of the scene and enhances their viewing attention;

2. It creates more power in the scene; and

3. It heightens the audience's kinesthetic connection with the actor.

First, regarding the audience's perception of time: just think of taking an unbroken trip on a freeway. It is seemingly endless, while an equivalent trip—taking exactly the same amount of time—but organized into detours, breaks, and rest stops (beats and transitions in acting terms) seems shorter. In a structured scene, therefore—once again as in the rule of life—the audience's sense of perceived time moves similarly more quickly—thereby creating greater audience intensification and excitement—while the absolute duration of a scene may remain constant or even increase.

Secondly, a structured scene increases performance power. Imagine a football or soccer field without boundaries or a game without rules. The lack of these structural elements diminishes the tension of the game. A structurally-restricted field of play, on the other hand, by having sidelines and goal lines and rules—thereby reducing the players' options— intensifies the emotional experience of their playing. Ordered, organized life is heightened life. Without a lid on a pot, the steam evaporates. Put a lid on it and you have a pressure cooker.

Thirdly, structure enriches the audience's possibility of kinesthesia, thereby enhancing audience self-recognition.

In the audience's everyday life, human structural rhythmic patterns abound. The human heart pumps blood through the arteries; it collects it back through the veins. People inhale; they exhale. They work all day; they sleep at night. They work all week; they get two days off. They work all year; they take a vacation. Rhythm—the structuring of life—is common to all human existence. When structured rhythm occurs in the actor's performance life—in the formal organization of scene activity—it enhances by rhythmic identification an audience's acceptance of the reality of what is happening, and thereby maximizes the audience's involvement.

Inherent Structure: Dialogue and Movement

Language, movement, and props themselves, as discussed earlier, are implicit structural components in a scene: they are the sculptural givens of the script. By their very nature, words, movement, and props are the outer shaping of inner impulses. They are inner emotion organized; shaped into outer action.

Actors are, therefore, automatically aided in their search for structural benefits in a scene by adhering to these structural contributions of writers and directors. Writers give the actor verbal structure; directors give them movement structure.

A smart, good actor—seeking structure in performance— should initially focus on becoming courageous enough, secure enough, and smart enough not to hamper the writer's and director's inherently structured (scripted and directed) offerings. Like a smart jockey with a great horse, the actor should often just get "on the script" and the director's blocking, mount the dialogue and other structural forms and rhythms of the scene, and just ride. Let the script-horse do most of the work: learn your lines as written, follow the director's blocking, use the suggested props in the script, and let the eventual performance rehearsals run toward the finish line along the implicit structural tracks of these inherited shapes.

Simply do as James Cagney is reported to have suggested to actors: "Just learn your lines, don't bump into the furniture, and never get caught acting."

"Beats" and "Transitions"

Beats and transitions are acting terms that remind actors to analyze, rehearse and perform a scene according to the innate logical and rhythmic forms inherent in dialogue.

A beat is a scripted group of lines or actions in a scene organized around a single unifying topic. For example, during an initial beat in a scene, the character(s) talk about going to the movie: what movie to attend, what time does it start, and whatever else they need to know about the show. Then a transition occurs, where the initial movie attendance topic ends and the next topic begins: whether they want to eat dinner before or after the movie, or where.

The characters discuss that for a bit, then a new transition occurs, followed by a new cluster of dialogue logic, or new beat: perhaps they have been fighting over the movie and dinner plans and, in the third beat, they discuss whether this is going to be their last date.

A transition is the emotional moment between the clusters of logic. It is generally accompanied by a time attenuation: a pause or sometimes a speeding up of the dialogue in reaction to what the other person has said. In either case it is a change of dialogue tempo and occurs when a character decides (generally unconsciously) that the initial cluster of tactical logic (the prior beat) was not securing him a victory—or the prior beat has secured him a tactical victory and it seems a favorable time to move on to another topic, another beat, in order to speed along toward overall victory.

Likewise, beats and transitions can occur in non-verbal physical actions in a scene—such as in a car chase or in prop action sequencing. The first beat in the car chase scene may be the initial chase phase; the transition occurs when the driver shakes the pursuer and relaxes to consider his next operational move. The new beat occurs in a renewed chase, to be culminated by the pursuing heavy driving the car off the bridge. The hero relaxes … transition … only to be chased again by another heavy's car … another beat.

In the case of props, the initial handling of the prop (for example, finding and sharpening a pencil) is the first beat; the transition occurs when the prop-handling actor, for example, ceases in his handling the prop in order to think. The next beat occurs when the character resumes his prop activity; perhaps starts tapping the pencil on the desk and then writing something on paper. He finishes, thinks again (transition); and then (new beat) starts fiddling with the prop in a new way, perhaps chewing on the end of the pencil, then (after a pause; transition) throws the pencil against the wall and walks out of the room. Another transition, a pause; then he re-enters the room to get his pencil.

These rhythmic patterns of beats and transitions—the inherent structure of a scene—aid in increasing audience-engagement … and stamina. Just as audiences in their everyday life need a balance between work and sleep, night and day, the ebb and flow of tides, they likewise need pauses in the ever-heightening intensity of the beats and transitions in the scene being viewed. They need time (moments of absorption) before the renewing the intensity of a new beat.

Without beats and transitions, the audience tires out. Too much unrelenting drama causes the audience to tune out; too little bores them. An excess in either direction—too many beats without transition, or too many transitions without intense engagement beats—produces audience detachment.

Beginning, Middle and End

Life has a beginning, middle and end; so must a well-acted scene.

A scene's events are born, they grow, and they die. Ideas are introduced, they expand, they conclude. Topics are established, debated, and then resolved. An initiating event happens, a complication occurs, a resolution is achieved.

This pattern of organized developmental change, a logical developmental progression from beginning to middle to end of a scene, is another structural component that makes an actor's performance ordered, compressed, rhythmic, powerful, and exciting. Good actors seek out this structural component in any scripted scene, and in performance strive to conform to it.

Character Development

"Character development" (sometimes called "character arc") is another common structural element in exciting acting. Character development is the personality structure of beginning-middle-end. The concept is that any character in a scene is revealed most exciting when he reveals himself developmentally throughout the scene. What the character's persona is at the beginning of the scene is not where it ends.

Another way to look at it is as an analogy used before: as characters engage in conflict, each layered character mask (of denial) is ripped away by the exigency of the conflict, forcing the truer and truer masks of the character's fundamental personality to be revealed as the scene progresses.

The good actor seeking character development often starts his character in the beginning of any scene emotionally as far removed as is logically possible from his emotional state at the end. For example: if the final outcome for the character in the scene is to be humorously buoyant, the actor is advised to consider starting the scene sad. If the character in the scene is to end suicidal, the actor might start the scene happy. If the character in the scene is to end confused, he might enter the scene certain.

Once again character development in acting is consistent with everyday life: many, if not all, people walk through their lives in initial states of denial, masking their true feelings, and these deep feelings are only revealed *ex post facto*, after the fact, when life's exigencies have ripped off the masks and forced their true feelings into the open.

This systematic developmental uncovering—slowly and periodically—of a character's essential and deeper personality during a scene aids the audience in its involvement by creating the possibility of character discovery, surprise, reversals of fortune, self-recognition and self-discovery, each of which, as we have noted in an earlier chapter, are always audience-compelling elements in a well-acted scene.

"I'm fine, Doc."

Similar to when I differentiated between the terms *technical* and *mechanical*, I am going to—once again—quibble over semantics: as a substitute for the term *character development*, I prefer the term *character revelation*.

Perhaps it is the cynic in me, but I don't think human character develops; it is increasingly revealed. People don't change; they get better at being the same.

No one wants to develop emotionally; they just want to succeed within their present masked state. Therefore, the use of the term *character revelation* is, for me, a truer expression of what happens in the process of personal evolution than the term *character development* because, as in everyday life, most discovered emotional changes are forced onto and therefore revealed by a character. Personal truth is exposed only when the masks are shucked aside under the blows and urgings of conflict. No one really wants to be unmasked, to know themselves. *Character revelation*, rather than *character development*, is a more proper term for this scaled mountain-of-last-resort.

A man goes to the psychiatrist and he says, "I'm fine, Doc. I had a pretty good week."

"Uh-huh," the doctor says, in typical non-committal fashion. The patient frowns; he is not getting from the doctor what he wants, which is to be told, "You're wonderful just the way you are!"

The patient is forced to continue, to reveal further. "Well, my mother died," the patient says. He sees the doctor frown. "But," he adds quickly, "we were expecting it. It was a painless death."

"Uh-huh," the doctor says. ("Uh-huh" is doctor-speak for "Bullshit!" Or, more kindly, "I don't believe a word you're saying. We haven't arrived at the heart of the matter yet.")

The patient reluctantly admits a new truth, "I did cry a little, but my eye doctor assured me the tear ducts can be repaired with laser surgery. No big deal."

"Uh-huh."

After a long pause, "All right; I used to hate her when I was a kid. You know, she used to beat me," the patient confides.

"Uh-huh."

The patient stands up, punches the wall. "Bitch!" He kicks the wall. "She deserved to die. Fuck her! I'm glad she's dead!"

"Uh-huh."

The man finally falls to the floor, crying. "I miss her! I miss my Mommy!" The doctor calls the ambulance.

The patient's character didn't develop, but his true character was increasingly revealed.

Build

A build in a scene—the increasing intensity as the scene progresses—is another valuable structural component in a performance. It is created by the increasing energy a character expends in trying to win the scene's conflictual life without unnecessarily facing and revealing personal truth! In order to maintain involvement in the conflict, the character must, albeit unwillingly, dig deeper and deeper into the pockets-of-his-past, or inner emotional layers, be forced to discover deeper and deeper truths about his inner self, to be able to ante them up and stay in the game of conflictual life.

Earlier, I characterized each successive raise in a poker game as requiring a progressive commitment of more and more consequential funds to stay in the game. The first raise in the hand comes from less consequential earlier winnings because the player plays with "house" or casino money. The next raise comes from one's own discretionary funds, followed by putting the food money into the pot, then the mortgage payment, and ultimately borrowing from the bank and then from the in-laws. As each outflow of funds becomes more personally consequential and harder to commit to the game, personal stakes are raised and intensity of effort increases. As each raise is harder and harder to give over, it takes more energy to accomplish.

In acting, similarly, the characters in a conflictual scene are reluctantly forced to dig deeper and deeper into personal layers of truth to defeat the opponent. These truths emerge with greater intensity from the increasing depths of the actor's personality. In the process, innocence is reluctantly lost; often ultimately shattered. Shields are removed. Truth is stripped naked of artifice, and the emperor is revealed as without clothes. The climax comes from a final release of tension that has developed in a scene. The final explosive release of truth creates a beneficial or shattering burst of self-discovery, and the climax of victory or defeat.

"The ultimate weapon is maximum fire power, minimum delivery system: put the same amount of pressure through a narrower aperture and increase the power."

Chapter 10
Making Sure a Performance is Elegant

The writer Ernest Hemingway defined courage as "grace under pressure." In his own lifetime, Hemingway drove ambulances in war-zones during the Spanish Civil War; faced deadlines in the newspaper business; attended bullfights in Spain; participated in long drinking bouts with great matadors; fished in tumultuous seas; went on safaris in Africa; and hunted with big game hunters. Yet his prose style throughout his life was simple and elegant to the point of minimal. For his body of work (and to a greater degree his sparse style), he received the Nobel Prize in literature.

At the end of his life, however, facing pain, old age, and atrophying skills, he used a gun to blow out his brains. Some say in that final act he betrayed his own sense of courage and was graceless under pressure, while others say his end was short, direct, elegant, and unadorned. His death was simple and economical, powerful, and as stylishly direct as his prose.

There is no Supreme Deity of Acting who pronounces "Thou Shalt Be Elegant." The value of performance elegance derives from a pragmatic base, following a truth of physics. Economy in actions increases power: the power of an acting performance flows in indirect proportion to its area of release.

Unencumbered by fear, hesitation, clumsiness and doubt, the logically functioning human mechanism—and good actor—creates little wasted effort. She shepherds her resources; she overcomes obstacles with a minimum of effort. An elegantly operating human machine operates like a well-calculated internal combustion engine, using only as much gasoline (energy source) as it needs to keep the system running at the desired speed.

Only a fool—or a bad actor—pays more emotional energy than a given task requires. Good actors expend their energy in direct proportion to the job to overcome the oppositional resistance of their external reality. With an elegant actor, there is no grunt to lift a feather, no wasted over-effort to push a weakling.

Elegance (like all the other Elements in Exciting Acting) occurs naturally in life, arising from the human need for physical economy. Wasted effort is counter-productive to human long-term survival needs. The human machine has only so many revolutions in its lifetime of operation. It would burn up early—die young—unless it achieved its goals attended with elegance ... with economy.

Remember when you were a child playing in Mama's garden and Mama gave you an open water hose with which to play? When you wanted to shoot the water farther without turning up the water pressure, you put your thumb over the release hole. You howled in glee as the water spouted, perhaps far enough to douse your father or annoying baby brother. The same principle applies in great acting: an equal amount of pressure released through an ever smaller aperture increases the power throw.

Acting is Living

What the ever-common term "less is more" means is less diffusion of energy in the outer release of emotion equals greater power. To state it another way, focused energy creates power and authority.

Why should a writer use three words when one word expresses the same emotional essence? Why should the actor repeat a gesture when the first gesture encases the total emotion and more effectively makes the point? Why should the actor kiss with fury when a gentle touch to the lips, filled with the same passion, more than suffices? An excess of released actions undermines its effect, whereas economy heightens clout.

Engineers say a normal office building floor can support thousands of pounds of pressure exerted downward by a ten-by-ten foot steel plate. However, reduce the mass of the steel plate, condense it, concentrate the thousands of pounds into a smaller mass area, and the pressure of the concentrated steel plate smashes through the floor ... and through several floors below that! That is the concentrated power of condensed force ... and of an stylish actor.

In an elegant actor, the desired performance style can be considered maximum (emotional) fire power carried by the minimum delivery system: an atomic bomb restricted to the size of a pea.

A bad actor, on the other hand—one who is too eager to show off his acting prowess, who says with his body language "Let me show you how hard this action is—and how brilliantly able I am to accomplish it!"—exerts excessive and unreasonable actor's energy. He lifts the feather with a grunt, and pushes the 98-pound weakling with ferocity generally associated with extricating a two-ton truck out of three feet of thick mud. Such over-exertion (inelegance) is bad acting that generally comes from the insecure, overeager false actor who tries to push the audience to appreciation and applause with external-to-actor-energy, instead of creating where the proper energy in the scene should originate: character-driven—and reality-calibrated—emotional character necessity.

Insecurity and Inelegance

A champion boxer is often said to "slip" the opponent's best punches, such a wonderfully smooth word for such a silken defensive gesture. Watch how the experienced champion uses minimum effort to escape another boxer's blows, reserving energy for the counter punch, the full fury of which is directed in a short, economical distance of ten to twelve inches, "exploding"—another great boxing term that is applicable to good acting—on contact.

On the other hand, young and inexperienced boxers—like overeager young actors—often flail like windmills while trying to hit one another; their conflictual efforts produced—whether in the ring or on set—disproportionate to an opponent's resistance.

Experience has not yet taught these young actors how to handle great amounts of emotional pressure economically, to focus their energies, to shepherd their resources, and to react with direct elegance and precision under duress. Instead, their youthful eagerness, desire, insecurity, and fear overwhelm them. Their potential power, non-tempered as yet by experience, remains unharnessed, not yet forged into economy and elegance: it becomes wasteful.

Great actors, on the other hand, never seem to be "doing anything" in performance. The motto of a boxer some say was the greatest heavyweight boxing champion in the second half of the Twentieth Century, Mohammed Ali, "Float like a butterfly, sting like a bee," self-describes his style. While he moved and punched in the ring with the grace and elegance of a butterfly, by focusing his fury with elegance, he was able to hit his opponents with the controlled punching power of a bee's sting. An exciting actor does the same. He is an artist who has learned to be comfortable being uncomfortable under the deepest emotional exigencies; thus, he is able to be elegantly direct and powerful in his actions.

In the film *Chinatown*, the director Roman Polanski, who played a "heavy" (the bad guy) in the film, decides to beat up the leading man, Jack Nicholson, for the latter's unwanted and antagonistic involvement in Polanski's character's life and work. Filled with hate, Polanski, instead of choosing a two by four piece of lumber or a metal pipe to knock Nicholson unconscious, does something much more cruelly and memorably elegant: he takes out his small pocket knife, opens the slender blade, and slits the inside of Jack Nicholson's nose! (It *still* makes me shudder to recall.) What is more kinesthetically powerful: shooting someone with a cannon or sticking a small needle into the middle of their eye?

Subtle, elegant, well-acted performances like Polanski's take audiences out of their seats and up onto the actor's performance tightrope, forcing them to respond with the same emotional grace as the elegant actor. When the good actor does that, the audience is forced to move (uncharacteristically for them?) economically, carefully, step-by-step, elegantly across great emotional divides, intensifying and advancing their kinesthetic emotional involvement.

An exciting actor is a subtle, elegant tease, expending just enough of her inner and outer self to keep the audience interested; not so much they get bored, not so little that they get frustrated.

Elegant Acting and Unity

A bad actor who senses her performance lacks intrinsic emotional power often ostentatiously costume-jewels her performance with physical excess. She exaggerates gestures and underscores her dialogue and movement with extra actor energy. She moves and speaks as if she's dressing her performance with baubles and beads. Her face contorts with effort. The brows furrow ("You see how hard I and my character are trying to win, and how difficult all this is?"), and her voice squeaks with muscular effort.

Such inelegant actors remind me of writers who know their written sentences lack intrinsic power and substance, and therefore put far too many of their words in "CAPS," repeat them, add exclamation points to everything they do. In their behavior they are cousin to the bad actor who underlines a failing performance with excessive expressive effort.

Why do bad actors—or bad writers, for that matter—act in such a manner, ornamenting their performances with rococo flourishes, thereby dissipating and wasting their creative energy? Are they intrinsically bad actors, or are they just trying to be bad actors, not knowing the difference? My guess is that in all bad acting efforts they are trying to compensate for a lack of emotional involvement in the scene.

When an actor is feeling insufficient inner emotion required for an exciting performance—let's say half of what he thinks is desirable or possible in performance—the bad actor often encourages himself to double his outer expression to compensate for his lack total emotional involvement. He thinks he will achieve the full power of a performance according to the following formula: ½ feeling x 2 (double expression) = 1. Since the number 1 is the mathematical symbol of unity, it becomes the symbol of a whole performance the actor tries to achieve. Unfortunately, creating actor-imposed, overly energetic compensation for the lack of full inner feeling results in bad acting.

The best corrective action to this form of bad overacting—exaggerated outer behavior to compensate for deficient inner feeling—is for the actor to feel more deeply. I remember the delight I experienced as a child while playing with plastic ducks in the bathtub. When I wanted to make the ducks jump higher out of the water, I held them more deeply underwater: the deeper the duck was held, the higher it jumped when released. Just so in good acting: when the actor experiences an honest depth of feeling—when the actor feels the full totality of the emotion she desires appropriate to the size of the gesture she requires—she no longer needs to compensate for the emotional deficiency by doubling the expressive component of her performance. Acting with deep emotional honesty best achieves the desired state of true acting elegance: 1 (deep emotion) x 1 (proportional expression) = 1 (powerfully elegant performance).

For the mathematicians and economists among you readers, allow me to graph the above:

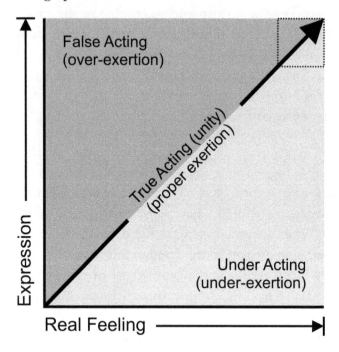

1. When the bad actor over-exerts herself, operating in the False Acting area to the left of and above the graph's Unity Acting line, the corrective is to increase her real feeling to justify the desired size of the expression, or to reduce the expressive size to conform to her honestly felt emotion ... thereby bringing total performance to a state of unity; or reality.

2. When the under-actor operates in the area to the right and below the Unity Acting line, the following corrective applies: this actor must open up—increase—physical expressiveness to match real feeling, or decrease the real feeling to match the under-expressiveness of her physical exertion ...

in either case bringing total performance to a state of unity; or elegant reality.

3. When the actor operates on the Unity line, however, that actor is an elegant actor, matching expression to real feeling. To become an exciting actor, she must move ever farther out on the Unity line, maintaining reality while increasing the performance to one of greater feelings *and* greater expression.

A GRAND, GRAND SUMMARY
The Ten Essential Elements Reviewed:
Parts I and II

Our review of the ten elements of exciting acting is now complete: **Conflict, Reality, Honesty, Interdependence, Audience Witnessing, Intensity, Variety, Complexity, Structure,** and **Elegance.**

A good and exciting actor must recognize that greater excellence in any part or scene—or, for that matter, in a career—will not be achieved by altering the formula, leaving out any of the Ten Elements, or including any new variables. Rather, excellence is achieved by raising the exponential power of any and/or all of the ten variables, applying each and/or all variables with greater effectiveness and efficiency.

Good acting becomes:

$$A + B + C + D + E + F + G + H + I + J;$$

Better acting becomes:

$$A + B + C + D + E + F + G + H + I + J;$$

Best Acting becomes:

$$A + B + C + D + E + F + G + H + I + J;$$

Brilliant acting becomes:

$$A + B + C + D + E + F + G + H + I + J.$$

Preparation for the Job

FedEx delivers the script to my house. I read it diligently, devouring all the dialogue and stage directions. I vow to live the role, so I automatically decide I am going to transform myself emotionally to walk excitingly in the shoes of the character.

Cliff Osmond

I begin my analysis and preparation according to the ten elements of exciting acting. However, unlike the writer of this book, I start my script analysis with character: eggs ahead of the chicken, emotion over shape, character over plot. As I said in the introduction, acting is a circle, subject to being entered at any point … so I can start my acting preparation at wherever point of the circle I like, as long as all other points within the circle are touched in final performance.

Starting with character, and in seeking to grasp the character demands in the script, I use information gathered from the script's dialogue, stage directions, and my imagination to work on the emotional prior history of my character, including past relationships.

I supplement this with other actor-preparation techniques, such as emotional recall, sense memory, substitution, and the moment before, to begin to activate a specific and destabilizing emotional subtext in me logical to what my character wishes to say and do in the scene in the pursuit of victory.

Furthermore, I maximize character importance (intensity), variety and complexity—and make sure to include elements of opposites, counterpoint, and contradiction—to further fuel my subsequent actor-as-character exciting performance.

Now … strongly emotionally destabilized, I define my objective in the scene, a goal that I, as character, consciously or unconsciously feel will best stabilize me in the future. I ensure my goal is simply-defined, all-inclusive, fundamental, active, solution-seeking and non-judgmental (as to propriety, possibility, productivity, and rationality), and make sure all the scripted dialogue, movement, facial reactions, prop use, and thoughts conform to the logic of my character's stated-goal/purpose. I make sure to maximize the conflictual tension of my goal, as opposed to the other character(s) goal(s), by making my objective very important to me: I will fight to achieve victory.

Next, I consider the sculptural shape of the scene's actions, one that best organizes the audience's perception of my on-stage/on-set performance. In the dialogue, I hunt for beats and transitions, beginning, middle, and end, and character development. I appreciate—and promise to ensure—that the intensity I feel during the scene will build reluctantly during the scene due to my holding down (through denial, self-obfuscation) the costs of self-revelation, and thereby increase my energetic commitment to winning.

I remind myself that all structural form will arise in performance emotionally and organically pursuant to goal.

Finally, I vow to create my performance with economy and elegance, and perform in a manner and style appropriate to character, place, epoch, and dramatic genre ... and vow to win the scene through the other person at all costs.

Through this constant and committed preparation work in rehearsal, I am confident I have absorbed and learned—gotten into my unconscious muscle memory—all dialogue, movement, prop use, desired emotions—and trust that the script's movement suggestions and my desired blocking have taken care of the audience's witnessing needs.

My character/plot preparation is now complete.

Performance

I appear backstage or on set.

Just prior to the performance, waiting in the wings or waiting for the cameras to roll, I fine tune my emotional susceptibility with a final emotional exercise or two, polishing and maximizing my emotional destabilization.

I next vow to enter the scene with no special prescience of the past, present, or future. I vow to be aware of no special resonance or meaning. I will have no idea what may or may not occur in my subsequent performance. I'm not even expecting much of a performance life. I expect it to be a short scene.

Cliff Osmond

I will, of course, win, but, at the same time, I will contain the possibility of losing.

While anticipating brevity in the scene, I have prepared myself emotionally to have the capacity to endure if victory so dictates.

I will commit one action at a time. I expect the world, moment by moment, to fall at my feet. I will be taken aback if that doesn't occur.

I will not play result, anticipate, or end-game the performance.

I expect to win easily, quickly, and cheaply, and through the other person.

As a final preparation check, I look at the particulars of actors-as-characters preparing to enter the scene with me: their hair, their face, and their body. I thereby make them become real to me. I promise to look and listen to them during the scene, and taste, smell, and touch them and the other particulars—inanimate as well as animate—that arise in the scene. I remind myself that, in performance, my dialogue and other actions will never release emotion for its own sake, but I will always convert into specific actions any emotions the other person stimulates in me; actions that will convince these other characters to accept my point of view. I will strive mightily to achieve the other person's admission of defeat, and will not stop unless someone lowers the curtain or says "Cut."

Conflictual
Real
Honest
Interdependent
Witnessed
Intense
Varied
Complex
Structured
Elegant

254

Acting is Living

The checklist is now complete. I am ready to act.

No! Wait! Not yet!

"Prior to performance, immolate the actor and allow the character to arise phoenix-like from the ashes."

Addendum
"Kill the Actor"

The greatest toxin to living an exciting performance is actor self-awareness.

After rehearsal and immediately before you walk on stage or on set, forget all you have learned about acting, including everything written in this book, including everything about the character and your subsequent performance you decided and worked on at home or on set. Forget your rehearsals and preparation. Dismiss from your mind all conscious knowledge of acting, including awareness of the coming scene—anything to do with acting, and trust that all your study and scene preparation is in your muscle memory!

The great classical guitarist, Andre Segovia, when asked how he avoided artist self-consciousness during performance, explained that while in rehearsal, he built the music's scaffolding. He constructed a conscious platform from which he shaped and guided what he was musically building. However, once the performance began, he had to remember to take the scaffolding down. He had to remind himself to forget his preparation and rehearsal— to have confidence that he prepared properly—and in performance just enjoy playing the music.

Stanislavski said, "The good director dies within the actor."

I would like to add: "The good actor dies within the character." Remind yourself that you have been hired to live the life of the character, not the actor; to walk in the character's shoes, not your shoes.

Actors often say, "I've got to get the audience." I rebut: You don't have to "get" the audience: they are already yours. They came a long way by car, bus, and Metro just to see you. You are situated in the light; they are in the dark. They have left their work at home; they have turned off their cell phones and have nothing else to do but watch you. Their attention is totally on you ... and will remain there, on you, as long as you don't lose them, which will not happen as long as you remain confident and exciting.

Preparation is over. You are now the engaged character. Thank the actor in you for his conscientious effort in preparing you and dismiss him from your arena of concentration. If he balks, fire him. All right: keep him on retainer if you wish, but bring him back only if problems arise. Remember that you are no longer an actor: you are now the character.

Beware the Head

Actor consciousness, once released during performance, has a tendency to stay open, like Pandora's Box, which is why actors should not be thinking of their dialogue during performance! When that occurs, only the ill winds of bad acting escape. The good actor should always follow James Cagney's great dictate for actors: "Learn your lines, don't bump into the furniture, and never, never get caught acting."

To paraphrase from the words of the social scientist Abraham Maslow, the exciting actor must now move in his rehearsal and preparation from unconscious incompetence (the initial reading of the script) to conscious incompetence (the early stages of conscious rehearsal discoveries) to conscious competence (the final rehearsals) to unconscious competence (the performance).

Descartes said, "I think; therefore I am," but the good actor in performance must disagree with the French philosopher. The good actor must say, "I am; therefore I think." Good actors remember that real acting is experiential, not analytical. Final performances best exist clear of conscious thinking or control.

I like to offer actors the definition of spontaneous in the Merriam-Webster Dictionary because it is an exemplary essay on great performance acting.

> Main Entry: **spon·ta·ne·ous**
> Function: adjective
> Etymology: Late Latin *spontaneus*, from Latin *sponte*, of one's free will, voluntarily
> Date: 1653
>
> 1. proceeding from natural feeling or native tendency without external constraint
> 2. arising from a momentary impulse
> 3. controlled and directed internally: **self-acting** <*spontaneous* movement characteristic of living things>
> 4. produced without being planted or without human labor: **indigenous**
> 5. developing or occurring without apparent external influence, force, cause, or treatment
> 6. not apparently contrived or manipulated: **natural**

Finally: Yogi Berra, a Hall of Fame catcher who played with the New York Yankees in the early and mid-1950s, was a great, free-swinging, and instinctive batter. However, he was notorious for swinging at bad balls (that is, balls pitched outside the strike zone). In spite of that flaw, however, he batted over .300 most years (the usual cut-off point for batting excellence). In an effort to increase his batting average, his coach, Casey Stengel, told him to "think" at the plate. "Don't just go chasing bad balls, Yogi. Think; think where the pitch is located before swinging."

Yogi dutifully went to the plate, bat in hand, poised to swing. The pitcher threw. Strike one. The pitcher threw again. Strike two. The pitcher threw a third time. Strike three. Yogi never took the bat off his shoulder. When he returned to the dugout, Casey glared at him: "What the hell are you doing up there? I told you to think."

Yogi responded, "You want me to hit or you want me to think? I can't do both."

Think before you act, think after you act, but when you act, just live.

Now... you are ready to perform.

About the Author

Cliff Osmond is a veteran actor, director, writer, and teacher based in Los Angeles, CA. He is a long-time member of the Academy of Motion Picture Arts and Sciences (the Oscars), the Academy of Television Arts and Sciences (the Emmys), the Screen Actors Guild (SAG), American Federation of Television and Radio Artists (AFTRA), and the Writers Guild of America (WGA). As an actor, Cliff guest-starred in over a hundred episodes of network television shows and TV movies of the week, and he has co-starred in dozens of feature films.

Most notably, Cliff appeared in four Billy Wilder films, including starring roles in *Kiss Me Stupid*, with Dean Martin and Kim Novak, and *The Fortune Cookie*, with Jack Lemmon and Walter Matthau, who were Cliff's sponsors into the Motion Picture Academy. Cliff also wrote and directed *The Penitent*, starring Armand Assante and Raul Julia.

A graduate of Dartmouth College with a BA in English, Cliff has an MBA in Finance from UCLA. He also advanced to candidacy for his PhD in Theater History from UCLA. In fall 2004, he served as Adjunct Professor of Acting and Resident Artist (Directing) at Georgetown University.

Cliff has taught 20,000 students in a career that extends over 40 years. He presently teaches acting and scene study in Los Angeles. For more information, please visit Cliff's website: *www.cliffosmond.com*.

CPSIA information can be obtained
at www.ICGtesting.com
Printed in the USA
LVHW110155030619
619866LV00001BA/312/P